Gender-Responsive Standards and Assessment Tool (G-SAT)

Handbook

AND

Trauma-Informed Practices for Working with Girls

Staff Handbook

Oregon Coalition of Advocates for Equal Access for Girls

Gender-Responsive Standards and Assessment Tool (G-SAT)

Handbook

Oregon Coalition of Advocates for Equal Access for Girls

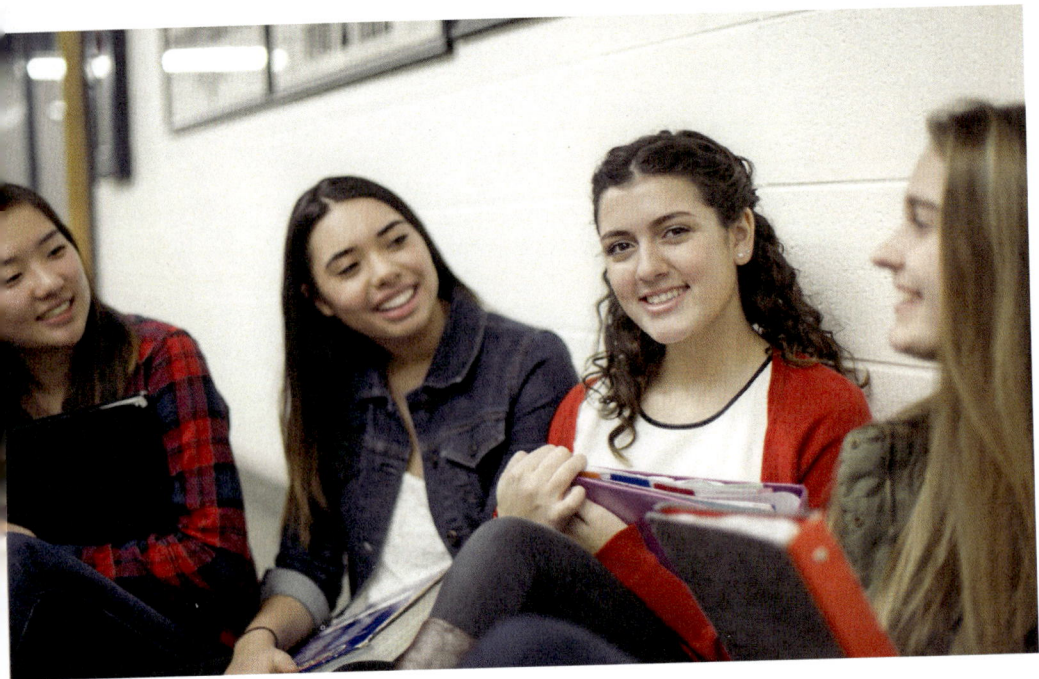

Table of Contents

Acknowledgements

Thank you to all the individuals and agencies that helped in the development of the <u>Gender-Responsive Standards and Assessment Tool</u> (G-SAT). This handbook was the creation of the Oregon Coalition of Advocates for Equal Access for Girls. Since 1993, the Coalition has been committed to advocating for girls' equity in access to all the gender-responsive support and services they need to help them to develop to their full potential.

Thank you to Pam Patton and Marcia Morgan for creating, developing and writing the original *Guidelines to Gender-Responsive Programming for Girls* in 2000 and *How to Implement the Guidelines* in 2002. Their vision for the specific things girls' programs need and how to get there never wavered. The Guidelines set the foundation, along with a national review of related documents, for the development in 2011 of the <u>Gender-Responsive Standards and Assessment Tool for Girls' Programs</u> (G-SAT) for staff and girls. The G-SAT is a comprehensive instrument that was developed incorporating best practices and the most empirically sound standards.

Thank you to Sarah's House, Oak Creek Youth Correctional Facility for Young Women, and the Salvation Army White Shield Center for Girls who were willing to be pilot sites and to assist in the development process of the G-SAT. Their feedback was beneficial as the tool was refined to be user-friendly and to best meet the needs of girl's programs.

Thank you to Jeannette Pai-Espinosa, President of The National Crittenton Foundation and Jessie Domingo Salu, Vice President of The National Crittenton Foundation. Their guidance, support and steady encouragement helped these tools advance.

The design and initial printing of the *G-SAT Handbook* was produced with support from a grant to the Coalition of Advocates for Equal Access for Girls from the OJJDP's National Girls Initiative.

Thanks to the Coalition's NGI Project Steering Committee: Maria Chavez-Haroldson, Mandy Davis, Terry Ellis, Faye Fagel, Javelin Hardy, Susan Mahoney, Shannon Myrick, Judge Adrienne Nelson, Melissa Spalinger and Shannon Wight who gave constructive feedback in the development of this handbook. Their expertise provided an academic, research-focused, pragmatic and diverse lens to ensure the handbook was clear, gender-responsive, culturally sensitive and trauma-informed.

Thank you to Marcia Morgan, Ph.D. for writing the *G-SAT Handbook* so that a variety of programs can easily access this essential information and use it in the most effective way. And thank you to Jude Baas for his invaluable editing contribution.

Finally, a big thanks to Pam Patton, Coalition founding member, president for 20 years and current State and National Liaison for the Oregon Coalition of Advocates for Equal Access for Girls. Her perseverance, drive, passion and direction made this Handbook happen in Oregon and potentially nationwide. She has been the strongest advocate for girls and this project with her heart always focused on what will make Oregon, and the nation, a better place for girls and young women.

Foreword

Why can't I reach this girl? Why is my program helping some girls, while other girls continue to fall through the cracks? Why can't the system affect even more girls positively?

Our goal with this handbook is to help you to answer these questions. So that every girl who finds her way to you can have the chance to become empowered and move forward successfully; to not be disadvantaged by the circumstances that brought her to your program, but instead to be herself, to develop to her full potential and to thrive.

In the 30-plus years I have worked as an advocate, this is the message I received over and over from girls who had been through the system: *One person cared about them, one individual in their lives understood and accepted them, was there for them and believed in them; that is what made the difference.*

The girls in your program come to you with complex lives, from multifaceted family and community situations, complicated by traumas, social influences and historical forces, and it can feel at times like you have little or no control on how you or your program will ultimately impact them.

This Handbook sets the groundwork for its complementary partner, the *Trauma-Informed Practices for Working with Girls—Staff Handbook*, and was developed to give you the strategies and tools needed to reach girls where they are at, to see them more clearly through a "gender lens," and to help them in their journey to self-determination, empowerment, belief in themselves and success.

A gender-responsive and trauma-informed approach is essential for both girls and boys. In this Handbook we focus on the girls.

To learn more about the benefits of a gender-responsive approach when working with boys and young men, I recommend Dennis Morrow's *the Male Box*. Dennis is Executive Director of Janus Youth Programs, Portland, Oregon, and his DVD series is a fundamental resource to programs and systems that serve boys and men (for more information, I encourage you to visit equalaccessforgirls.org/the-MaleBox).

This is not easy work. We know it takes passion and commitment, and it takes an understanding and knowledge about what is effective with girls. Our hope is that this Handbook can help by giving you the foundation needed to adjust your lens, and affirm that what you're doing is the best approach you can use in working with girls.

So that one person she needs to find is YOU.

—Pam Patton
State and National Liaison and president for 20 years of the Oregon Coalition of Advocates for Equal Access for Girls

Why Your Program Should be Gender-Responsive

Why Should You Care About Being Gender-Responsive?

A wide body of research suggests that a successful program must acknowledge and address the fact that the needs of girls differ from the needs of boys, and therefore must take those differences into account.

The road to adulthood for girls involves different challenges and developmental experiences than that of boys. Their psychological and social perspectives, environmental and cultural influences, and developmental needs often differ significantly from those of boys and young men.

A gender-responsive approach works effectively for both girls and boys when designed specifically to meet their unique characteristics and needs.

Girls face eating disorders, depression, violence and abuse, homelessness and prostitution, and run away more frequently than boys.[1] Girls and boys are socialized differently and experience and respond to events differently. They have different pathways to problem behaviors, and while facing similar challenges often face them differently.

Girls differ from boys in their relationships, cultural roles, communication and learning styles, and the experiences they bring with them to your program.

Girls come to the attention of Juvenile Justice and the social services system differently than boys:

- Girls frequently "visit" delinquency through status offenses or misdemeanors, and often have only a brief initial encounter.

- A girl's first contact with Juvenile Justice or law enforcement is more often for behavior that would not be considered criminal if committed by an adult.
- Girls rarely enter or end up in the Juvenile Justice system for violent or person-to-person crimes.
- If/when girls go deeper into the system; often it is for violations (of probation/parole), not more severe offenses—boys' progression more often involves an escalation of offenses and reoffending.

A gender-responsive approach for girls allows a program to respond effectively to these differences.

Who are the Girls in Your Programs?

The girls in your program have experienced trauma.

- Justice-involved girls and boys experience trauma at rates that are 8 times higher than community samples and the statistically significant gender differences in the prevalence of trauma, its impact, and its type and treatment necessitate a gender-responsive approach.[2]
- Girls are three times more likely than boys to have experienced sexual abuse, which is often an underlying factor in high-risk behaviors that lead to delinquency. It is estimated that 70-90 percent of girls in the Juvenile Justice system have been victims of sexual abuse.[3]
- The age at which girls are at greatest risk of sexual abuse victimization is puberty, around age 14. Boys are at greatest risk between 6-10 years old and even then their risk is only half that of girls of the same age.[4]
- National surveys of adolescents in the general public indicate that one out of four girls have been sexually assaulted. Over one-half of the women who have reported being raped at some time in their lives were under 17 years of age at the time of the rape.[5]
- Abused and neglected girls are twice as likely to be arrested compared to non-abused girls, and 2.4 times as likely to commit a violent offense. For 40% of girls arrested, those arrests are for sex related offenses, such as prostitution. (It should also be noted: 70% of abused girls do not go on to be arrested for criminal acts.)[6]

The girls in your program are increasingly involved in the Juvenile Justice System.

- Arrests of juvenile females have been steadily increasing nationally since 1993, more than juvenile male arrests in most offense categories.[7]
- Although violent crime arrest rates have declined for both females and males since peaking in the mid-1990s, the number of girls being arrested, detained and placed under Juvenile Justice supervision has been steadily increasing, running counter to trends for boys.[8]

The girls in your program are challenged by substance abuse (alcohol, tobacco, and drugs).

- 51.4 million (or 42 percent) of females age 12-18 report using an illicit drug at some point in their lives.[9]
- The National Survey on Drug Use and Health indicated that 61 percent of surveyed girls age 12-18 (74.5 million girls) had used alcohol during the previous year.[10]
- Girls' non-medical use of prescription painkillers, alcohol, and methamphetamines matches or exceeds boys.[11]

The girls in your program are vulnerable to homelessness, running away, and sex trafficking.

- 61 percent of runaways are girls, and girls serve twice the amount of detention time for status offenses compared to boys.[12]
- The most frequent age of entry into the commercial sex industry in the US is between 12-14 years of age. Each year in the US, between 100,000-300,000 children, mostly girls, are trafficked. Runaways, the poor, and girls are the most vulnerable.[13]

The girls in your program struggle with mental and emotional health.

- Female youth offenders have higher rates of mental illness than male youth offenders. In the general population, girls have higher rates of what is called "internalizing mental disorder" (e.g., depression, anxiety) while boys have higher rates of "external" disorder (e.g., ADHA, conduct disorder, behavior problems).

- Girls suffer from depression more than boys, and by mid-adolescence girls are more than twice as likely to be diagnosed with a mood disorder (girls are also more likely to seek help). Depression can affect school performance, relationships, and physical health. One in four girls fall into a clinical diagnosis (e.g., depression, eating disorders). Many more report being anxious, sleep deprived, cutting, other mental/emotional disorders or other serious pressures.[14]

- 5% of girls and women have eating disorders (vs. 1% of males). 50% of teen girls and 30% of teen boys use unhealthy weight control behaviors. 90% of all teens with eating disorders are girls. There has been a rise in anorexia in young women ages 15-19 in each decade since 1930.[15]

- Suicide is the third leading cause of death for girls ages 15-24 in the US. Girls tend to attempt suicide by drug overdose or poisoning, or by cutting themselves. Girls think about or attempt suicide about twice as often as boys. (Boys die by suicide four times as often as girls.)[16]

- Seven in ten girls believe they are not good enough or do not measure up in some way; including looks, performance in school and relationships with family and friends.[17] And 78% of girls who are 17-years old are "unhappy with their bodies."[18]

In the context of gender-responsive programming, girls learn how to manage their assets, develop the skills to negotiate those assets in relationships, and learn skills that enable them to live as autonomous, self-directed human beings.[19]

Definition of a Gender-Responsive Approach

Often a girl will come to you in a state of fear, powerlessness, dysfunction and helplessness; and her problem/destructive behaviors carry with them a high societal cost.

Our systems have yet to incorporate the connection between how our culture values and invests in the needs of girls and the cycles of abuse, violence and crime, and implicit bias. Therefore, it is imperative that those of us who work on the front lines of child and youth services include a gender-lens and gender-responsive approach.

National statistics show that girls need and currently lack specialized, gender-responsive services to help them overcome their barriers to success.

A gender-responsive approach will:

- Better match your program's services to a girl's needs.
- Enable your program to work more effectively with girls, build trust, and impact their futures.
- Equip your system's organizational structure, culture and practices to better support and assist girls.
- Empower your program to be more successful in helping girls reach their potential.

By creating a safe, gender-responsive context for them, while restoring their power and value as individuals, your program will more effectively and consistently succeed for girls.

Rather than an "add-on", a gender-responsive approach is a universal framework that demands specific adjustments to the practices, policies and culture of your organization. It is integrating an understanding of gender throughout your system of care.

Being gender-responsive means that a program's policies and practices recognize that girls and boys have different needs and responses to their life experiences and form relationships differently; and for your program to be effective it must address these differences.

Race and ethnicity, sexual orientation, gender identity and class also have a significant collective effect on girls. A foundational awareness of this intersectionality is essential to the gender-responsive shaping of your program, and how you perceive, respond to and affect girls and young women.

Having a gender-responsive approach for girls means:

- Basing the delivery of services upon your knowledge of a girl's life and experiences, and the holistic understanding of the impacts that they've had.

- It is providing all staff with the gender-responsive and intersectionality awareness, skills and knowledge needed to successfully support girls.

> A gender-responsive approach celebrates and honors girls' unique experiences, understands and considers environmental and societal impacts on girls, respects and takes into account female psychological, physical, emotional, and social development, and empowers girls to reach their full potential.

A gender-responsive approach for girls includes:

- Intentionally allowing gender identity and development to affect and guide your services and practices.

- Being receptive to the issues and needs of being a girl and valuing the female perspective.

- Creating a physical, social, emotional, and spiritual environment that reflects and understands the reality of girls' lives.

Being gender-responsive means:

- Ensuring that your program environments and services are welcoming, engaging and appropriate for girls.
- Taking time to allow for relationships and trust to develop.
- Looking at and understanding what girls have experienced prior to entering your program, and seeing their behavior through a "gender lens."

Gender-responsive programming takes gender into account as an important factor when considering what kinds of services and programs need to be available and how and where those services should be delivered.

It is your choice of strategies and methodology, tone, intent, and your sensitivity to a girl's world and the high probability that she has experienced trauma.

Being gender-responsive does not mean:

- Painting the walls pink, either literally or figuratively.
- Taking a co-ed program or a program currently for boys and making it girls-only.
- Creating "gender-neutral" programs that do not address the specific risks and needs of girls. (Gender-neutral programs often are developed based on theories/research done on the dominant or larger research population, which is predominantly male.)

Gender-responsive programs support self-determination, and focus on empowerment and helping girls to find and use their voice.

When your program is gender-responsive, it will:

- Provide girls with safe and socially appropriate opportunities to speak up and advocate for their own opinions, beliefs, and rights.
- Inspire girls to embrace their individual strengths, skills and abilities.
- Encourage girls to understand and trust their own feelings, intuition, opinions and intellect.
- Embolden girls' natural spirit, creativity and innovation.

Through a gender-responsive approach your program will:

- Create a context that is physically and emotionally safe for girls, with transparency, predictability and clear and consistent boundaries with staff.
- Value the individual girl, with respect, authenticity, collaboration, compassion, mutuality, and relationship.
- Restore personal power to girls, giving them choices, internal strength, skills building, and positive modeling.
- Generate a culture and environment that addresses the whole girl, holistically considering the complex intersectional influences and realities of her life.

When your program is gender-responsive it will provide safe opportunities for girls to address how to develop healthy male and female relationships, how to heal from trauma and abuse, how to succeed in school and work, and how to plan for the future.

Being gender-responsive means that your program responds to the unique needs of the girls and young women you serve.

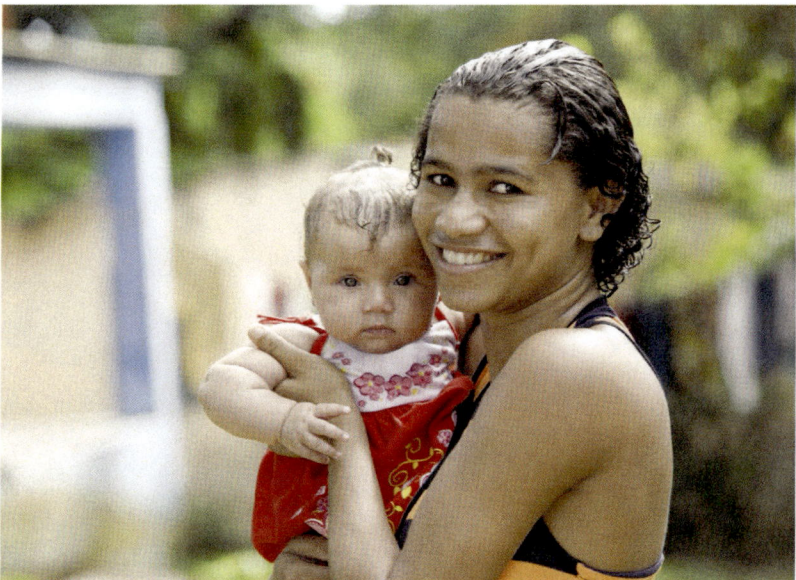

Six gender-responsive principles for justice-involved girls:

1. *Acknowledge that gender makes a difference* (there are differences between boys and girls; their world view, their socialization, their needs, and what works better for each sex)

2. *Create an environment based on safety, respect and dignity* (this will help girls thrive, be more cooperative and be better able to work towards their goals)

3. *Develop policies, practices and programs that are relational and promote healthy connections to family, significant others, friends, their child if they have one and the community* (since girls value relationships, this is fundamental to their success)

4. *Address substance abuse, trauma, and mental health issues through comprehensive, integrated and culturally relevant services and appropriate supervision* (these three areas are interconnected for girls; so all need to be addressed together, not in isolation)

5. *Provide young women with opportunities for potential improvement in their socio-economic conditions* (this can be a real and/or perceived roadblock; SES—Socioeconomic Status improvements help girls to succeed)

6. *Establish a system of community supervision and re-entry with comprehensive collaborative services* (girls are more likely to succeed with a structure and transition plan that is built on relationships)

These six principles are a valuable guide to help all programs, systems and agencies serving girls and young women to establish a foundation upon which gender-responsive programming can flourish.[20]

Passion for Your Work and a Gender-Responsive Program Culture

This work is hard and rewarding.

> *To do this work requires a genuine passion for what you do and that passion comes from knowing and feeling that your work and efforts matter.*

That passion then increases your positive impact on the girls.

Before incorporating gender-responsive programming, take the time to ask yourself a few questions. This will help both line and administrative staff to be more mindful and purposeful and consequently more successful with the girls in your program.

Ask yourself…

- Why did I get into this work?
- What motivates me? What gets me up every morning, excited to face the day?
- Do I have a personal commitment to justice and fairness for girls?
- Can I see the goodness in girls who may not act lovable, or who have been rejected by families and society?
- Do I believe that a gender-responsive approach can work?
- If I had to guess, how do I think my coworkers would answer these questions about me?

Then ask yourself these questions about your surroundings, program culture and your environment:

- What do I hear administrators and/or co-workers say about the girls with whom I work?
- Is what my administrators and/or co-workers say positive or negative? Is it productive or destructive to the culture, to staff, and to the girls in the program?
- What is the culture of my program?

Culture change can come from the top down or bottom up.

You can have an impact on your program's culture by changing the words used and energy supported, and then by helping others to do the same.

Do you ever hear co-workers or administrators in your program say these or similar things:

- Girls have the courage to share their feelings (vs. girls are whiny).
- Girls want to change, and girls crave role models (vs. girls are needy).
- Girls are survivors who have lived through difficult situations, ones where they were not respected and their communication role modeling was not healthy (vs. girls are manipulative).
- Girls express themselves verbally and connect and build relationships through talking, which is great for staff because we always know what is going on (vs. girls talk too much).
- Our program wants to do what works for girls to help them succeed, and that is why we embrace gender-responsive best practices. (vs. gender-responsive programming is not "real" corrections or justice work).
- Working with girls is rewarding; when you help a girl you are helping generations (vs. nobody wants to work with the girls, girls are too hard; I only work with girls because there weren't any other openings).

Negative statements and misconceptions or destructive labels and framing can lock your program and staff in an unproductive spiral, and can create an environment that is not productive for girls or for program staff.

Without a positive culture, gender-responsive programming will have a challenging time becoming incorporated.

When your culture begins to see girls through a gender lens, their behaviors make more sense. Consequently, program staff will see their work and their approach with girls differently.

With increased understanding, staff can be more positive and targeted in what they do. By meeting girls' specific needs and creating positive outcomes for them, a culture with a gender lens is more effective in reaching them.

With a gender lens your program will be more successful.

Integrating a gender-responsive culture and approach does not mean treating boys and girls identically. In fact, the opposite may be true.

> Because a boy's program gets $100 to buy camping equipment, does the girl's program have to use their $100 to buy camping equipment as well? (No, unless the experience or adjunct result of camping is something the girls need.)

> Do program girls have to have the identical calorie count in their meals as the boys? (No, unless their physical demands require it.)

> Because the boys' recreation area has weights starting at 25 pounds, do the girls' weights have to start at 25 pounds too? (No, and the recreation area may be more effective for girls if they don't.)

> Because a girl's program gets money to buy art supplies to make a family memory book, does the boy's program have to use their money the same way? (No, unless that project will productively resonate with what the boys are working on.)

How programming monies are spent, like other program decisions and practices, should be gender-responsive, not identical.

How and Why the G-SAT was Created

The Background and Development of the <u>Gender-Responsive Standards and Assessment Tool</u> (G-SAT)

The Coalition of Advocates for Equal Access for Girls

In 1992 the Oregon Coalition of Advocates for Equal Access for Girls (the Coalition) was created when a group of concerned, experienced child, youth and family services professionals formed a statewide advocacy organization with the purpose of ensuring girls equity in access to services and that they have the opportunity to develop to their full potential.

In 1993, the Coalition introduced and helped pass in the Oregon Legislature the Equal Access Law for girls (ORS 417.270). As a result, Oregon is the only state in the nation with a law that requires all state agencies that provide services to children ensure that girls have "equal access to appropriate gender-specific services, treatment, and facilities."

To this day, the Coalition continues to support professionals and non-professionals who empower girls, and advocates for and educates people and programs about all girls 9-19 years of age, especially those who are at risk for endangerment and disconnection. It remains an all-volunteer, member-driven organization dedicated to ensuring that the needs, issues, and voices of girls are heard.

> *The Coalition is an information resource on the issues that girls face, an education resource on how to effectively work with girls, a network supporting those committed to helping girls, and a state level advocate for girls and gender-responsive programming.*

Because our goal is always to help girls become healthier, and more self-sufficient and reliant, to be better citizens and have better self-esteem, to be better communicators and thrive outside the system, we are all obliged to step back and ask:

- *Why are we doing things the way that we are?*
- *Is the way we are doing things working or not working for girls?*
- *Could how we are doing what we're doing work better, be more effective and have better results if our programming were more gender-responsive?*

The G-SAT's Original Sources

Past Coalition sponsored publications preceding the G-SAT include: *Oregon's Guidelines for Effective Gender-Specific Programming for Girls* (2000) and its accompanying manual, *How to Implement Oregon's Guidelines for Effective Gender-Responsive Programming for Girls* (2002).

Each of these publications provides information and suggestions to assist programs that work with girls and young women in their creation of gender-responsive design, practices, services and programming.

The interconnected gender-responsive guidelines assemble to create a program environment that can enhance and maximize your effectiveness for girls, the goal being not to change "what you do," but to guide you "in how you do it."

What we know is that when your program is set up to meet the needs of girls, the undeniable result is more positive outcomes.

The guidelines are applicable to a wide variety of services; from community-based prevention programs for girls at-risk, to intensive residential programs, detention, and state institutions for girls and young women.

The Creation of the G-SAT

In 2011, the Coalition received a grant from the Meyer Memorial Trust to build upon the work of the original gender-responsive guidelines contained in *How to Implement Oregon's Guidelines for Effective Gender-Responsive Programming for Girls*.

After an extensive national literature search we were able to compile the most empirically sound best practice standards from various tools, including *Oregon's Guidelines*, to create a comprehensive instrument that was then refined, piloted with staff and girls, and developed into 59 gender-responsive standards for residential programs for girls.

This led to the creation of the first <u>Gender-Responsive Standards and Assessment Tool</u>, the <u>G-SAT for Girls' Residential Programs and Services</u>, which includes both a *Residential Programs Management and Staff Tool* and a *Residential Programs Girls Tool* (2011).

Two more G-SAT's were later developed; the <u>G-SAT for Girls' Therapeutic, Treatment, and Proctor Foster Homes and Services</u>, which includes a *Foster Home Parents Tool* and *Foster Homes Girls Tool* (2013), and the <u>G-SAT for Girls' Community Programs and Services</u>, which also includes both a *Community Programs Management* and *Staff Tool* and a *Community Program Girls Tool* (2016).

These 3 G-SAT's are designed to help programs and services that work with girls and young women to assess and improve their gender-responsive effectiveness.

By educating your program about and then measuring and evaluating how your program meets each gender-responsive standard, these G-SAT's create a foundation of information and provide the opportunity to improve services and enhance your program's or system's support and outcomes for girls.

After which, the assessment standards' components provide your program with an essential resource and baseline strategy to help you maximize and sustain your program's success through maintaining each of the gender-responsive standards.

The Purpose of the G-SAT

The purpose of the G-SAT is to improve the foundation, quality, nature and effectiveness of the services your program and system provides to girls, thereby increasing girls' chances for success and self-sufficiency.

Although gender-responsive can refer to meeting the programming needs of either girls or boys, the focus of the Gender-Responsive Standards and Assessment Tools (G-SAT) is program standards for girls.

> The G-SAT's are designed to ensure that every program serving girls has the foundation required to provide and integrate effective and consistent gender-responsive services, and to enable programs to create a culture, environment and strategy that best supports its girls and staff.

The **G-SAT** *Management and Staff Tool* provides your program an essential assessment tool and resource of clearly stated gender-responsive standards, each with specific, outlined components describing how management and staff can help your program meet that best-practice standard.

And...

The **G-SAT** *Girls Tool* gives the girls in your program a "voice" and the opportunity to share how your programming or services are working for them, and simultaneously provides you with the indispensible resource of girls' input.

Using these G-SAT tools will:

- Enhance the ability of your program or services to assess how it is meeting gender-responsive standards and how it is working for girls.

- Provide your program with an ongoing resource of clearly stated gender-responsive best practice standards, each with clear components that outline how to meet the standard and increase program effectiveness.
- Develop and convey a comprehensive evaluation picture of your program or services; revealing through the correlation of the *Management and Staff Tool* and *Girls Tool*, a roadmap of actionable steps toward better results for girls.

How the G-SAT Works

There are three different G-SAT versions for programs or services that work with girls:

1. G-SAT for Girls' Residential Programs and Services: which includes both the *Residential Programs Management and Staff Tool* and *Residential Programs Girls Tool*. (This G-SAT is meant for residential programs and facilities, including Juvenile Justice, Child Welfare, mental health, and substance abuse programs.)

2. G-SAT for Girls' Therapeutic, Treatment, and Proctor Foster Homes and Services: which includes both the *Foster Home Parents Tool and Foster Homes Girls Tool*.

3. G-SAT for Girls' Community Programs and Services: which includes both the *Community Programs Management and Staff Tool* and a *Community Program Girls Tool*. (This G-SAT is meant for all non-residential and non-foster care programs.)

Each of the G-SAT versions has two tools: one for program line and leadership staff to complete (the G-SAT *Management and Staff Tool*) and one for the girls in the program to complete (the G-SAT *Girls Tool*).

The G-SAT's survey format and design are unique but comparable for each of the two program or system populations that will complete the tool (*Management and Staff and Girls*). The sections and questions within each tool are designed to correlate according to the best practice standard being assessed. This means that they can be used together for a comprehensive program evaluation and/or for specific standard and section performance comparisons during the tabulation of your G-SAT surveys from both groups.

> **The G-SAT *Management and Staff Tool*:** Examines four program areas from the perspective of management and staff. *Facility, Staffing, Programs and Services*, and *Administration/Leadership*. It is to be completed by all or a selected sample of management and staff (director/manager/superintendent and line staff—preferably no less than 10% of your staff who work with girls) in your program.

- The Tool is divided into four sections based on the program areas examined.
- The Area Examined is stated in bold at the top of each section (*Facility, Staffing, Programs and Services*, and *Administration/Leadership*).
- The Standards are numbered and delineated in bold within each area, with their descriptive components listed below them. Each standard's list of specific components is to be considered when that standard is scored on a scale from 1 to 10—10 being the highest.
- The complete tool should take management and staff approximately one hour to complete.

> **The G-SAT *Girls Tool*:** Examines three program areas from the girls' perspective: *Facility, Staffing*, and *Programs and Services*. It is to be completed by all or a selected portion sample of the girls in your program.

- The Tool is divided into three sections based on the program areas examined.
- The Area Examined is stated in bold at the top of each section (*Facility, Staffing*, and P*rograms and Services*).
- The complete tool should take girls approximately one half hour to complete depending on their reading level.

- The Standards are numbered and conveyed in an age-appropriate way, and use a different rating scale than the *Management and Staff Tool*. Whereas the staff score each standard on a 1-10 scale, best practice standards listed for girls are in "I" statements about how they feel or what they observe (e.g., "I feel safe in the building"). Rather than being labeled specifically within each area, the core essence of each standard is presented as a question/statement, which the girls then answer with a *yes, no, sometimes* or *not applicable (N/A)*.

- Much shorter than the *Management and Staff Tool*, the *Girls Tool* also includes the opportunity for the girls in your program to respond to two open questions. *"How do you feel this program has been helpful to you, and why?"* and *"Are there other things you would like to tell us about this program?"*

- Girls should complete the assessment tool individually, not in consultation with others, and should be given approximately one-half hour for a full G-SAT survey.

- If the entire population of girls will not be completing the assessment tool, the representative sample should include girls who are at different points (new, mid-point, near completion) and levels of the program.

- It is important to ensure anonymity and confidentiality for each girl.

  - When using a printed (paper) tool, have each girl seal her completed assessment tool within an individual, unmarked envelope. Then have her deposit that envelope into a larger collection envelope, which you have provided.

  - When using an on-line survey service or software, ensure that the service you choose and the access to a computer allows for and protects each girl's anonymity and confidentiality.

The *Management and Staff Tool* and *Girls Tool* for Your G-SAT

The G-SAT for Girls' Programs—*Management and Staff Tool*:

The following is a sample portion of the four sections of the *G-SAT Management and Staff Tool for Residential Programs*.

These samples are brief excerpts from each section area included in the complete tool—*Facility, Staffing, Programs and Services,* and *Administration/Leadership*.

Using each best practice standard's list of components as a guide, a representative portion of your program's management and staff score each standard on a scale from 1 to 10. (NOTE: For a more specific and in depth examination of a single section area, your management and staff can score each standard's component individually—the average of all component scores equaling an overall score for that standard.)

The first section of Standards in this *Management and Staff Tool for Residential Programs* sample is the *Facility*.

Facility

Standard	Score
1. The facility is a respectful environment. • Facility is clean, well lit, comfortable (e.g., temperature), organized, and well-maintained.	
2. The facility is physically safe for girls. • The physical structure where girls meet or reside is a safe place where they feel protected from violence, physical/sexual abuse, and other harm. • The facility space meets conditions of a suicide prevention/safe place. • The design of the facility reduces risk to girls and staff. Unsafe areas are identified (i.e., poor lighting, hidden or isolated areas) and the issues are addressed through such things as frequent staff checks, higher staff/girl ratio, locks, fire exits clearly marked and unobstructed, cameras and monitors. • If surveillance cameras are used, it is specified by whom and when it is monitored.	

3. **The location of the facility accommodates girls' lives.**	
• Facility is located near the communities from which the girls came. • Facility is easily accessible by mass transit.	
4. **The facility offers a female-friendly environment.**	
• Facility is welcoming to females with a comfortable visual environment. Colors are calming. Things such as posters, pictures, books, audio-books, magazines, DVDs, CDs, and wall decorations value females, are inspiring and empowering, and highlight positive female achievements. Advertising and other images are healthy messages for girls. • Facility does not have materials or play music that normalizes or glorifies violence against women, or reinforces gender role stereotypes. • Facility has a display board or something similar that features daily inspirational messages made by positive female role models. • Facility has areas where social activities can occur for girls to foster healthy relationships.	

The second section of Standards in this *Management and Staff Tool for Residential Programs* sample is *Staffing*.

Staffing

Standard	Score
11. **Staff are clear about their roles and boundaries with girls.**	
• Staff roles and responsibilities are clearly defined and include gender-responsive practices. • Staff understand and follow program policies and procedures. • Staff are trained and understand how to maintain their professional boundaries. • Male staff are aware that young women are often socialized from an early age to seek male attention. • Staff work as a team—recognizing the importance of each person's role in supporting girls' growth. • Staff are consistent with their message (rules, guidance, etc.) to girls. • Staff understand the importance of relationships in girls' lives and work to develop trust, maintain physical and emotional safety, and engage girls therapeutically for the purpose of facilitating individual growth. • Staff understand the legal consequences of engaging in sexual behaviors with girls and obligations of reporting. This includes familiarity with the Prison Rape Elimination Act that covers juvenile facilities, mandatory child abuse reporting laws, etc.	

Standard	Score
15. Staff exhibit healthy attitudes around girls. • Staff and administrators are gender-responsive in all actions and words. Staff are held accountable for their behaviors. • Staff are upbeat, positive, and optimistic. Staff do not use profanity, demeaning language, gender stereotypes, threatening language, or slurs. • Staff exhibit sensitivity to sexual orientation. • Program provides guidance to staff on how to recognize their own biases in their work with girls and if change is needed. • Staff take the physical and emotional safety of the girls seriously. • Staff do not use their job responsibilities as a reason to avoid being with the girls. • Staff connect well with the girls.	
16. Staff use gender-responsive communication skills with girls. • Staff use "relational language" not "rules language" with girls, other staff, and in program materials. Relational language is more personal, less authoritative and less threatening. It states what is needed rather than what cannot be done. It describes to the girl what is being requested in relationship to others, herself and the person making the statement. • Staff use relational practice by validating girls' feelings, using reflective listening skills, and developing trust. • Staff use respectful, non-sexist language with the girls. • An atmosphere of openness and discussion with the girls is encouraged. • Staff utilize affirmations, reinforcing and encouraging words instead of confrontational language.	

The third section of Standards in this *Management and Staff Tool for Residential Programs* sample is *Programs and Services*.

Programs and Services

Standard	Score
17. Programs and services are relationship-based. • Healthy relationships and positive connections are at the core of the program, from intake to aftercare. Program embodies an understanding of the significance of relationships and connections in girls' lives. • Program acknowledges that attachment, interdependence, and connectedness form much of the foundation of female identity.	

- Program helps girls see any connections between their relationships and their involvement in the juvenile justice system. Girls are prepared and supported when separating from unhealthy relationships. Staff understand that girls generally won't give up unhealthy relationships until they create healthy relationships.
- Girls learn to appreciate and respect themselves rather than relying on others for validation.
- Program is aware that a girl might view establishing goals leading to her independence as undesirable when it appears that it will result in breaking off relationships and connections to others.
- Staff are trained on how and when disconnection from girls can and should occur.
- Staff connect and form a relationship with a girl so she trusts staff and does not feel alienated in the program.
- Program treatment groups are small and girls are given one-on-one time to build relationships with staff and other girls.
- Programs build in social time for girls to learn how to develop healthy relationships.
- Staff are aware of the impact trauma has on a girl, the importance of rebuilding trusting relationships, and avoiding re-traumatizing her through their words and behaviors.
- Program teaches girls how to identify and prioritize authentic, healthy relationships. Program educates girls about the dynamics of abusive and coercive relationships.
- Program differentiates between having healthy relationships and dependency. Issues of male dependency are addressed.
- Staff shifts the girls' primary focus and sense of identity away from male relationships. Staff addresses girl's value system that often prioritizes male relationships over female relationships.
- Program addresses the dynamics of gang affiliations or strong delinquent peer groups.
- Program addresses a girl's behavior in the social context of focusing on the choices she has made, both positive and negative.
- Program provides activities to build healthy relationship skills through female issues groups and group therapy. Staff discuss and model healthy female-female, male-male, and male-female relationships that are respectful with genuine concern.
- Connections to family are explored and strengthened if appropriate.
- Program offers groups that discuss how and why girls sabotage relationships, explore safe and unsafe relationships, reduce competition and cruelty with other females ("relational aggression"), and provide activities to build healthy relationship skills.

20. Programs and services are strength-based.

- Program staff addresses behaviors from a strength-based position (as opposed to deficit-based/disease model approach).

- Program works on a girl's power within, not over someone else. Program emphasizes girl empowerment, not submission to artificial rules and norms, so a girl can take charge of her life.

- Program focuses on earning not losing privileges and responsibilities. Program is based on providing a structure and guidance rather than punishment.

- Program works with a girl from the point where she is in her life. Program builds upon girls' existing strengths and understands how to help girls internalize (own) their successes, instead of externalizing them (credit others). Girls develop competencies that promote self-sufficiency. Staff focus on girls' strengths and enhance girls' skills to empower them to make healthy decisions and use their inner wisdom.

- Girls gain confidence/competence in new areas that build self-esteem, self-efficacy, a sense of control in her life, and help build positive social behaviors.

- Program provides leadership opportunities to girls (i.e., leading activities) and experiences of success.

- Program expects and encourages girls to succeed. Program focuses on positive rewards rather than the avoidance or elimination of negative consequences.

- Program tries to help girls shed negative labels (e.g., acting out, manipulative, bitch, "borderline" and other mental health labels).

- Program allows girls to learn from their mistakes.

- Program offers graduated opportunities for independence and decision-making.

- Program fosters positive identity development.

- Staff uses strength-based language and labels, such as "at-promise" vs. "at risk" girls, "powerful voices" vs. "loud voice", "negotiator" vs. "manipulator."

22. Program and services are holistic-based.

- Program addresses the whole girl within her social context (her relationships, socio-economic status, culture, media, peers, spiritual practice, family, school, home, social services, juvenile justice, education, social/emotional supports, etc.).

- Program deals with the causes, and not just the symptoms, of the girl's problems.

- Even when a girl's needs are prioritized, a view of the whole girl is kept in mind.

The fourth and final section of Standards in this *Management and Staff Tool for Residential Programs* sample is *Administration and Leadership*.

Administration and Leadership

Standard	Score
54. Agency/Organization has a gender-responsive philosophical foundation and mission.	
• The agency/organization's philosophical foundation and culture is gender-responsive. The program administration and leadership value and honor the female experience and allow gender to affect and guide services.	
• The agency/organization's foundation incorporates program practices that are trauma-informed, relationship-based, strength-based, and holistic (social, emotional, cultural, physiological), includes current gender theories on addiction, pathways to criminality, and incorporates research on female development, risks, needs, and strengths.	
• The agency/program's philosophical foundation matches actual practice. The gender-responsive approach is consistent from the top down.	
• Administration/leadership understands, accepts, supports, and is committed to a gender-responsive approach.	
• Administration recognizes that program's assumptions on girl's behaviors and needs must come from a gender-responsive and evidence-based perspective (grounded in research on female psycho-social development and gender differences).	
• The agency/organization supports a continuum of gender-responsive programming and services from intake to aftercare.	
• The mission statement clearly reflects beliefs, values, goals, and philosophies that are gender-responsive.	
55. Agency/organization has policies that are gender-responsive.	
• Policies include guiding principles and program values that respect female needs and experiences.	
• Policies are in writing, are known by staff, and integrated into all parts of the program.	
• Policies include a process for updating and changing with input from staff and girls.	
• Girls are represented on the board of directors or advisory boards for the agency or program.	
59. Administration addresses any gender bias in system.	
• Decision points in the system are reviewed for gender bias and gender-related barriers for girls.	

The G-SAT for Girls—*Girls Tool*:

The following is a sample portion of the three sections of the *G-SAT Girls Tool for Residential Programs*.

These samples are brief excerpts from each section area included in the complete tool—*Facility*, *Staffing*, and *Programs and Services*. Girls answer each question in the three sections with a *yes, no, sometimes* or *not applicable (N/A)*.

The first section of Standards in this *Girls Tool for Residential Programs* sample is the *Facility*.

Facility

Standard	Yes	No	Sometimes	N/A
1. I feel the space where our program is located is clean, comfortable, and organized.				
2. I feel safe in the building.				
3. I feel like the environment is for girls, not boys.				
4. There is comfortable space for my family if they come to visit me.				
7. I get some personal space where I can have my pictures or listen to music.				

The second section of Standards in this *Girls Tool for Residential Programs* sample is *Staffing*.

Staffing

Standard	Yes	No	Sometimes	N/A
8. Staff understand me and understand girl's concerns.				
9. Staff are respectful of girl's bodies. There are rules about unsafe touch and physical contact that are followed by staff.				
10. I trust the staff.				

	Yes	No	Sometimes	N/A
11. Staff understand and are respectful of my race and culture.				
12. Staff understand and are respectful of my sexual orientation, gender identity.				
13. I have opportunities to tell what I like and do not like about the staff.				
14. I have opportunities to tell what I like and do not like about the program.				
15. Staff are positive and respectful to me and other girls.				
16. It is easy to talk to staff and to understand their expectations of me.				

The third and final section of Standards in this *Girls Tool for Residential Programs* sample is *Programs and Services*.

Programs and Services

Standard	Yes	No	Sometimes	N/A
29. I feel safe from hurtful words and actions from other girls in the program.				
30. I feel safe from hurtful words and actions from staff in the program.				
34. I understand how my actions and my past impacts why I am here in the program.				
35. I understand it is important to help restore the harm I have done to others.				
46. If I get angry, staff teach me how to recognize, reduce and re-direct my anger.				
50. The program helps me in my relationships with other girls and women in my life.				
51. The program helps me in my relationships with males in my life.				
49. I have learned how to respect others.				
50. The program helps me feel more confident in my abilities.				
54. I feel like I have a good transition plan for my care after I leave the program.				

Each *Girls Tool* also includes its two open-ended questions:

1. *How do you feel this program has been helpful to you, and why?*

This question is meant to give girls the opportunity to dig deeper into the impact your program is having in their lives.

2. *Are there other things you would like to tell us about this program?*

This final question offers girls an opportunity to discuss all of their concerns, from food to visitation, to staff they don't like, etc., and is often a catalyst of rich information about your program, which might otherwise never have been revealed.

These open-ended questions are meant to provide valuable information, from the girls' perspective, to empower management and staff to adjust programs as needed; while also ensuring that each girl has the opportunity to express themselves outside the limitations of standardized statements.

Your program's leadership is encouraged to seize any opportunities for growth, strategic planning and quality improvement or assurance that this information provides.

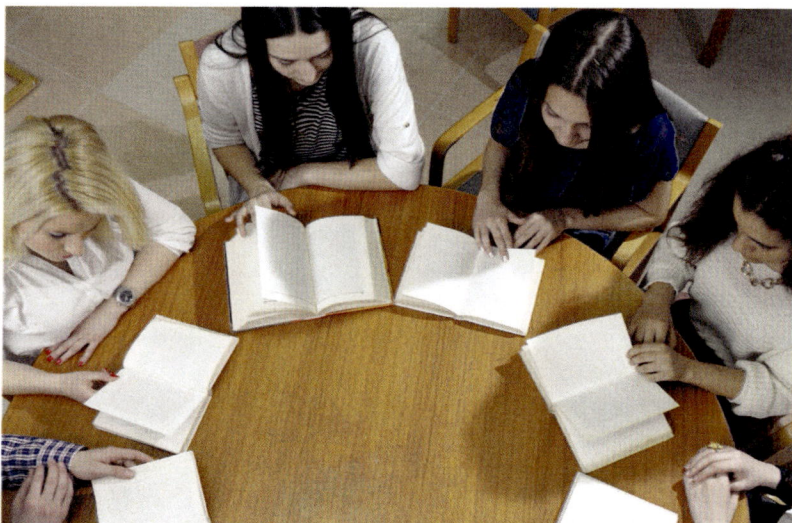

Why and How to Use the G-SAT

Why your Program Should Integrate the G-SAT

The G-SAT is valuable to your program in two indispensable ways:

First, it is an essential Assessment Tool:

> The G-SAT enables your program to assess how gender-responsive your facility, staffing, and services are for girls, and how effectively these areas are being administered; and it assists your program in establishing the culture and training necessary to manage your meeting of evidence-based, best-practices standards.

> G-SAT scoring will give a clear indication of gender-responsive standards that are or are not being adequately met by your program, and component scorings can then provide detailed information regarding specific areas where changes need to occur to better meet best-practices and improve effectiveness with girls.

> G-SAT scores provide an important opportunity for staff discussions about how your services compare to best-practice standards and how changes can greatly improve your outcomes with girls; while simultaneously giving support and positive recognition to the areas where your program is already succeeding.

> And scoring your G-SAT *Girls Tool* gives leadership, management and staff a more accurate and inclusive view of how girls are experiencing your program, in general and in relation to each area and specific standard.

Second, it is a fundamental <u>Resource</u>:

> The G-SAT itself, with its detailed list of standards and standard components is a key source of foundational information for your program. These standards and their accompanying components allow you to identify specific needed improvements, and what those improvements areas might effectively look like.

> The detailed programmatic information and comprehensive outline of specific gender-responsive methodology, services and programming within the components themselves can often be enough to shift your systemic and cultural practices and get your program headed in the right and most effective direction.

> Integrating your G-SAT results and gender-responsive standard component guidelines into your program's culture and strategies, through leadership and staff discussions, is one of the key steps toward becoming a successful program for girls.

On-line or Paper Version

Some programs prefer to put the G-SAT on-line for staff and girls to complete, using an on-line survey service or software. If there is a large number of staff and/or girls in your program, this may be the more desirable method, because the on-line survey service or software will both track the G-SAT survey entries and tally the results for you. Staff and girls will also be able to complete their on-line G-SAT on their own timeline and schedule.

- If your program chooses to put the G-SAT survey on-line, it is advisable to have staff and girls complete it in one sitting and on a device that has a reliable internet connection. Staff and girls may not be able to save incomplete surveys on the software option you choose to use, and poor or interrupted cellular/Wi-Fi connections may erase their progress.

- Also, as mentioned previously, be sure that the on-line survey provider or software you choose is able to protect/preserve staff and girls' anonymity, and that all staff and girls completing a G-SAT survey have access to a computer.

If you choose to administer a paper version of the G-SAT, be sure to allocate for additional time and the necessary materials, and also accommodate for confidentiality and anonymity, in both the filling out and tallying of the staff and girls G-SAT surveys.

The Importance of Anonymity

Because trust can be an issue for girls, and some staff in programs, be sure you have a structure in place to ensure anonymity when completing the G-SAT.

- Inform staff and girls ahead of time that their responses and comments will be compiled, to look for the themes and common suggestions that emerge, and that no name will be associated with any response.
- It is suggested that names not be written on individual copies of the G-SAT tool.
- As mentioned, if a paper version or your G-SAT is administered, also provide "privacy envelopes" in which girls and staff can individually seal their G-SAT survey, and a larger collection envelope for them to deposit it.

Special Considerations

Resistance

Some girls may resist participating in the G-SAT *Girls Tool*. Let them know that their opinions are valued, and encourage them to use their voice and be heard.

- Prior to administering the G-SAT, discussions should take place and information about the tool should be presented at staff meetings, so that all concerns and questions can be answered.
- The more involved staff are, in incorporating the G-SAT as both an assessment tool and a resource, the less resistance there should be from girls.
- You cannot mandate every girl in a program to complete a *Girls Tool*, but the more diverse the opinions and perspectives that you receive, the more accurate and powerful your results will be.
- Additionally, management should be involved in scheduling the time and place for staff and girls to complete the G-SAT.

Individual Effort

Some girls will be tempted to complete the tool in consultation with other girls or to talk about their answers as they fill out their G-SAT *Girls Tool*.

- As suggested, girls should complete their *Girls Tool* individually.
- Make every effort to give girls quiet, individual time to complete their *Girls Tool*, to ensure independent thinking and the voicing of their own ideas and experiences.

Discomfort/Triggers

Talking about difficult emotional situations can bring up significant discomfort, nervousness and challenging emotions, like sadness, anger, and fear.

- Prior to completing their G-SAT, let girls know who on staff is available to talk to them if they need help or support.
- Staff should be prepared if after completing their G-SAT girls are showing signs that the experience has brought up feeling related to trauma in their lives. These emotions could surface as acting out behaviors.
- Let the girls know that they do not have to deal with these emotions alone. Support/treatment options should be available.

How to Complete Your G-SAT: The Steps

There are 7 steps your program will take when completing your G-SAT.

Step 1: Decide on Format

- [ ] Decide whether you are going to be doing the G-SAT on-line or using a paper version.

- [ ] If using a paper version, set up a private/confidential means by which the completed G-SAT surveys are to be completed and submitted.

- [ ] If you decide to use an on-line survey service or software (e.g., Survey Monkey), the initial set up of the G-SAT will take some time, but your additional tracking and tally duties will be significantly reduced.

Step 2: Establish Staff and Girls' Buy-in and Trust

- [ ] Facilitate a discussion in a face-to-face meeting or similar setting, and reach a consensus with staff around the desire for the program to develop and provide the most effective services for girls.

- [ ] Describe the G-SAT and discuss how it is set up for both management and staff and girls to provide anonymous input.

- [ ] Emphasize that the standards are built upon best practices for gender-responsive services.

- [ ] Answer any questions or concerns and do "trust building" activities to ensure buy-in. Discuss the importance of trust when making constructive changes in the program and ultimately greater success for girls.

- [ ] Communicate to staff that their opinions are valued and will be heard, and the importance of their responses; and encourage them to complete their *Management and Staff Tool*.

- [ ] It will generally take one hour for staff to complete their assessment tool. They are asked to do so individually, not in a group and not in consultation with others.

- [ ] Leadership/management will need to create a plan to allow work time for staff to complete their G-SAT.

- [ ] Girls in the program typically complete their tool in less than 30 minutes. Likewise, girls are asked to complete their G-SAT tool on their own, and not in consultation with others.

Step 3: Administer G-SAT

- [ ] Set up a system to announce to staff and girls the intent, timeline and anonymity collection practices—such as a confidential drop box or collection spot for sealed envelopes.

- [ ] Distribute your paper or on-line G-SAT.

Step 4: Tally Data

- [ ] Tabulate and summarize the results. With a paper version of the G-SAT this can take several hours depending upon the number of completed assessment forms.

- [ ] Using an on-line survey service will decrease the tabulation and summary time.

Step 5: Establish Review/Advisory Team

- [ ] Select a team to review the data results and to make recommendations.

- [ ] Prioritize which standards or issues need to be addressed and in which order (e.g., safety issues, impact, effectiveness, ease in making changes, budget/cost).

- [ ] The review team should have broad representation and include administrators and line staff from different programmatic service areas.

- [ ] Ensure that both the information gathered from Management and Staff and from Girls is incorporated into any overall recommendations.

☐ Although the team may be ad hoc, with the task of synthesizing the responses, they can also play a long-term role in ensuring recommendations come to fruition.

Step 6: Determine Agency/Program Readiness

☐ When you learn that specific changes need to occur, stemming from your G-SAT results, your program should first determine your readiness for change. (Program leadership is encouraged to explore the vast amount of information available in change readiness literature.)

☐ Then ask...Are there specific cultural aspects that emerged from the G-SAT survey that need to be addressed within our program?

☐ Then ask...Are there training adjustments within our program that need to happen in order for change to occur?

☐ Readiness to change is a critical element to the success of incorporating new ideas and new ways to deliver and maximize your program's effectiveness.

Step 7: Maintain Quality Assurance and Follow-Through

☐ Establish a systemic plan, timelines and structured roll out for the changes you've designed.

☐ Then...Identify who will be responsible for administration and oversight.

☐ Adhere to your timelines.

☐ Finally, document and report all of your activities and gender-responsive changes. Administering this step may become the on-going role of the review/advisory team (mentioned in Step 5).

Scoring your G-SAT

How to Score your G-SAT *Management and Staff Tool*

When completing their G-SAT, staff is asked to only score the standard (which is in bold), using the components listed below it to help calculate their overall score for that standard. To ensure consistency, staff is asked to first read all the components before scoring each standard.

The following is the **1-10** scale used to score the standards.

1	2	3	4	5	6	7	8	9	10

Does not exist   Needs immediate improvement   Needs improvement   Needs little/no improvement

Score	Definition
10	Excellent, meets 100% of the standard's components, needs no improvement, opportunity to mentor other programs
9	Very Good, meets around 90% of the standard's components, needs little improvement, opportunity to work toward 100%
8	Good, meets around 80% of the standard's components, room for improvement, opportunity to refine effectiveness
7	Almost Good, meets around 70% of the standard's components, needs improvement, opportunity to increase effectiveness
6	Fair, meets around 60% of the standard's components, room for significant improvement, opportunity to improve outcomes
5	Almost Fair, meets 50% of the standard's components, needs immediate improvement, opportunity to transform outcomes
4	Poor, meets 40% of the standard's components, requires immediate attention, opportunity to crucially transform outcomes
3	Weak, meets 30% of the standard's components, requires immediate action, opportunity to make critical improvements
2	Very Weak, meets only 10-20% of the standard's components, critical failure, requires immediate management action
1	Non-existent or missing. 0% of component standards are met, complete failure, requires immediate leadership attention
N/A	Not applicable

What the Score Means

While you will get the most detailed benefit from your standard and section scores, your program's overall score can be determined by totaling the average score given to each individual gender-responsive best practice standard. The following chart provides a guideline for evaluating what that score means.

Grade	Score	Response
Excellent	475-590	Congratulations! A significant majority of the gender-responsive standards are in place and working great. Take note of any room for improvement; and remember to monitor your program, your progress/milestones, and to get continual feedback from girls and staff. Set a goal to improve even more! Mentor others.
Good	356-474	Your program has done well and has many of the gender-responsive standards in place, yet many still remain for you to integrate. Doing so will increase your success with girls and program effectiveness. Read the components listed below each standard for help and to further improve, and the literature to keep up on the latest research on best practices for girls.
Fair	237-355	You have made an effort to respond to girls' needs. Now onward and upward! Focus on building upon the standards you've met and integrating and strengthening those you haven't yet. Look at the components listed below each standard for specific ideas on how to meet/improve that standard. Once you do, you'll see increased success/effectiveness.
Poor	119-236	There are significant areas in your program that need immediate attention. Don't worry there are available resources to help you. First, start going through each standard and prioritize and strategize. Remember that the components listed below each standard will help you and give you direction.
Weak	0-118	Your program needs to immediately begin the process of unilaterally implementing gender-responsive standards. Resources exist to help you. Seek them out and don't be afraid to use them. Your success with girls and your program's effectiveness will begin to quickly improve once you do.

Looking Beyond the Overall Scores

> Once you have completed your G-SAT it is important to look deeper than your overall scores for your program and each section area. Close examination of your Management and Staff and Girls results, for each section and standard, will give you a better understanding of where your program is actually at, and will help you to identify areas that deserve celebration, need attention, require support, and demand improvement.

Review each Standard.

The average score may be high, but that does not mean there is not room for better outcomes within a standard.

- Look at the component statements listed below each standard to get specific ideas on how to improve and increase your program's effectiveness.

Many standards may need improvement, but scores that are 5 or below require your immediate attention.

Review each Section.

Total up the average scores for the standards in each individual section of the tool. Then compare your total score in each section with the maximum score possible.

- *Facility*: 8 standards, maximum score of 80
- *Staffing*: 8 standards, maximum score of 80
- *Programs and Services*: 37 standards, maximum score of 370
- *Administration/Leadership*: 6 standards, maximum score of 60

This will give you a picture of the section areas that need your attention most, and how to prioritize the standards you will focus upon first. Multiple sections may need to be addressed, but pay closest attention to those that have scores below 60% of the maximum.

How to Score your G-SAT *Girls Tool*

It is important to review your *Girls Tool* responses in a timely manner.

The G-SAT *Girls Tool* has a different scoring scale: *yes, no, sometimes* or *not applicable N/A*.

To score your G-SAT *Girls Tool*:

Tally each girl's response to each numbered question. (Almost every *Girls Tool* question number corresponds to a correlated standard number in the *Management and Staff Tool*.)

- For each *yes*, score the standard a 10
- For each *sometimes*, score the standard a 5
- For each *no*, score the standard a 0

Now calculate the average score of each standard (by adding all of 0's, 5's and 10's and dividing by the total number of respondents minus any N/A's). This is the overall *Girls Tool* score for that standard. (The score for each standard can then be used in comparison analyses to previous test group scoring, scoring from other programs, and to its correlating Management and Staff standards scoring.)

- If a standard receives an *N/A*, look for trends or consensus and areas that girls perhaps did not know how to evaluate, or did not realize are part of your program.

You can use this average score to rate your program from the girls' perspective on the 1-10 Management and Staff scale for each standard.

The *Girls Tool* questions are organized in parallel sections to the *Management and Staff Tool*. This gives you the opportunity to correlate and compared the Girls and Management and Staff results.

Girls may generally complete a paper survey. So, their answers will most likely be hand-tallied and/or then hand-entered if you are using an on-line survey service.

The detailed and overall information and correlations your program gleans from the *Girls Tool* should reveal the girls' perspective on your program and its effectiveness regarding fulfillment of gender-responsive standards. Their views may or may not be similar to management and staff's. Any variance can be just as useful as similarities.

Look for section questions that do not match management and staff's scores. Any area scored below a 6 should be immediately reviewed, discussed and improvements planned.

Give significant and focused attention to the girls' answers to their open-ended questions. Look for trends and correlations, and specific areas of success and need for improvement. Be especially attentive to any health or safety concerns or implications, and any information/testimony that requires immediate action.

Your first priority should be any standards that a majority of girls feel are not being addressed, or that are critical to their personal health and safety. These issues may need to be promptly addressed.

As with the *Management and Staff Tool*, it is important to look at your results in multiple ways: by cumulative score, individual sections, and by each standard, and ultimately by each component.

Training Resources

The National Crittenton Foundation can conduct an on-site training in your city or state, customized to meet your specific needs, on the G-SAT's gender-responsive standards.

Full trainings are typically one-day long, but are also available for half-day trainings and conference workshops. The audience can be as small as five or as large as 500.

For more information about on-site training, contact:

The National Crittenton Foundation
inbox@NationalCrittenton.org
www.NationalCrittenton.org

G-SAT Templates

For a copy of one or more of the three (below) G-SAT's for your program or programs, please contact the Oregon Coalition of Advocates for Equal Access for Girls at:

info@equalaccessforgirls.org

- G-SAT (R) for Girls' Residential Programs
- G-SAT (F) for Girls' Therapeutic/Treatment/Proctor Foster Homes
- G-SAT (C) for Girls' Community Programs

Oregon Coalition of Advocates for Equal Access for Girls
www.equalaccessforgirls.org

Endnotes

1   Hubbard, Dana Jones and Betsy Matthews (2008). Reconciling the Differences Between the "Gender-Responsive" and the "What Works" Literature to Improve Services for Girls. Crime and Delinquency, 54(2), 225-258.

2   Wolpaw, J.W., & Ford, J.D. (2004). Assessing exposure to psychological trauma stress in the Juvenile Justice population. National Child Traumatic Stress Network, www.NCTSNet.org

3   US DOJ "Research on Women and Girls in the Justice System" NIJ Research Forum, (2000)

4   National Center for Disease Control, "National Intimate Partner and Sexual Violence Survey", (2012)

5   US Department of Justice, BJS National Crime Victimization Survey, (2005)

6   US DOJ "Research on Women and Girls in the Justice System" NIJ Research Forum, (2000)

7   OJJDP Statistical Briefing Book, (2012)

8   OJJDP Statistical Briefing Book, (2012)

9   National Survey on Drug Use and Health, (2003)

10 Substance Abuse and Mental Health Services Administration, (2004)

11 SAMSHA, (2014)

12 OJJDP, NCJRS "Juvenile Offenders and Victims: 2006 National Report".

13 US Department of Justice, "Characteristics of Suspected Human Trafficking Incidents, 2008-2010" (April 2011)

14 Steven Hinshow, "The Triple Bind: Saving our Teenage Girls from Today's Pressures," (2009).

15 Hoek and Van Hoeken, (2003). Eating disorders are a daily struggle for 10 million females in the US. (SAMSHA, 2010)

16 Center for Disease Control, (2015)

17 Real Girls, Real Pressure: National Report on the State of Self-Esteem, Dove Self Esteem Fund, (2014)

18 National Institute of Media and the Family, (2009)

19 Hubbard, Dana Jones and Betsy Matthews (2008). Reconciling the Differences Between the "Gender-Responsive" and the "What Works" Literature to Improve Services for Girls. Crime and Delinquency, 54(2), 225-258.

20 Gender-Responsive Strategies: Research, Practice and Guiding Principles, National Institute of Corrections, (2003), Barbara Owen, Ph.D. and Stephanie Covington, Ph.D.

NOTES:

Trauma-Informed Practices for Working with Girls

Staff Handbook

Oregon Coalition of Advocates for Equal Access for Girls

The development, design and printing of the *Trauma-Informed Practices for Working with Girls—Staff Handbook* was funded through a grant to the Coalition of Advocates for Equal Access for Girls from the OJJDP's National Girls Initiative (2013-JI-FX-K007).

Table of Contents

Acknowledgements

Thank you to the National Girls Initiative for their support in the development of the *Trauma-Informed Practices for Working with Girls—Staff Handbook*. The handbook was the creation of Oregon's Coalition of Advocates for Equal Access for Girls (Coalition). Since 1993, the Coalition has been committed to advocating for girls' equity in access to all the gender-responsive support and services they need to help them develop to their full potential.

Thank you to Jeannette Pai-Espinosa, President of The National Crittenton Foundation and Co-Director of OJJDP's National Girls Initiative (NGI) and Jessie Domingo Salu, Vice President of The National Crittenton Foundation for their guidance, support and steady encouragement.

Thanks to the Coalition's NGI Project Steering Committee: Maria Chavez-Haroldson, Mandy Davis, Terry Ellis, Faye Fagel, Javelin Hardy, Susan Mahoney, Shannon Myrick, Judge Adrienne Nelson, Melissa Spalinger and Shannon Wight who gave constructive feedback in the development of this handbook. Their expertise provided an academic, research-focused, pragmatic and diverse lens to ensure the handbook was clear, gender-responsive, culturally sensitive and trauma-informed.

Thank you to Marcia Morgan, Ph.D. for writing the *Trauma-Informed Practices for Working with Girls—Staff Handbook* so that a variety of programs can easily access this essential information and use it in the most effective way. And thank you to Jude Baas for his invaluable editing contribution.

Finally, a big thanks to Pam Patton, Coalition founding member, president for 20 years and current State and National Liaison for the Oregon Coalition of Advocates for Equal Access for Girls. Her perseverance, drive, passion and direction made this Handbook happen in Oregon and potentially nationwide. She has been the strongest advocate for girls and this project with her heart always focused on what will make Oregon, and the nation, a better place for girls and young women.

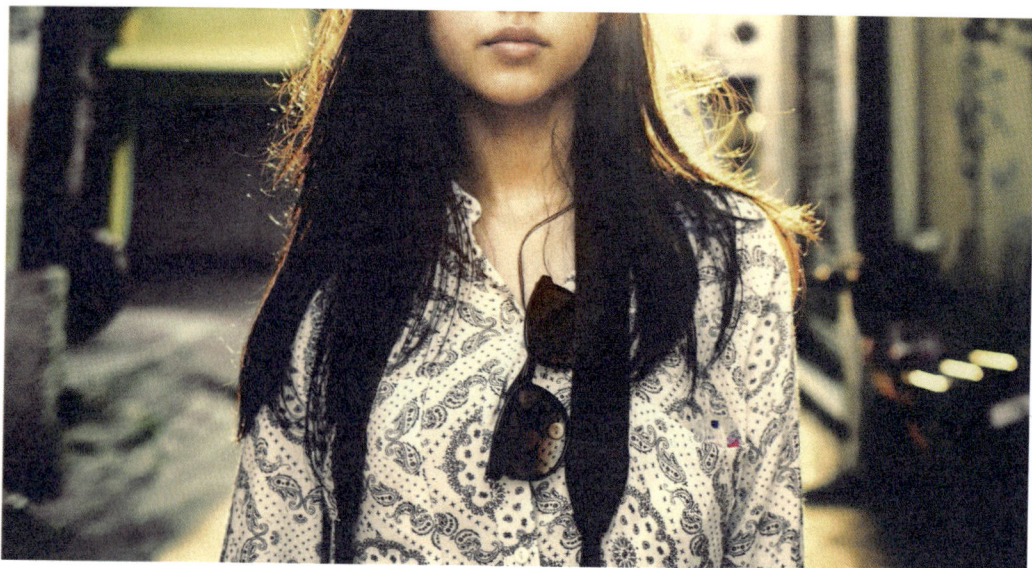

Foreword

What we know is that every girl in your program has experienced trauma. The truth is she has likely experienced many types, multiple times. She has survived sexual or physical assault, or rape; she's witnessed abuse and death, and has been touched by the effects of street violence; she has been affected by domestic violence and endured psychological, sexual or physical abuse; she's withstood the strains of poverty, neglect and abandonment; she knows the devastating hardships of historical and existing oppression, structural violence and racism. This is the girl who has found her way to you.

Trauma is destructive and it is pervasive in our girls' lives.

Trauma can overwhelm a girl's capacity to understand and integrate her choices or behaviors. It can create fear, powerlessness, dysfunction and helplessness. It can lower or corrupt her feelings of self-worth and hope. It can alter how she views herself, how she perceives the world and what she expects from her future. It can influence her emotions, actions, attitudes and reactions; and it can distort her outlook, impulses and her sense of self.

Trauma is the critical element shaping how girls will experience your program or system. To effectively work with girls, you must first understand trauma and recognize how trauma is impacting them. The girls in your program or system are the focus of this handbook, however, much of the information is relevant to boys as well. It is just as essential when working with boys that you understand the toxic, complex impact of trauma from the male perspective. Both girls and boys experience trauma far too frequently, the prevalence of the type and damaging results however differ.

We created this handbook to build upon our companion publication, the *Gender-Responsive Standards and Assessment Tool Handbook*. As with a gender-responsive approach, a trauma-informed approach means enhancing your effectiveness by mindfully addressing the specific, individual needs of the girls or boys in your program.

For girls, this means adapting your culture and awareness, and refining your strategies and practices to meet their unique characteristics and needs. It means being conscious of the interconnections of race, ethnicity, sexual orientation, gender identity and class, as a collective influence affecting how girls experience their environments and social contexts, and how they relate to others and themselves.

A trauma-informed approach means grounding all aspects of your program in an understanding of trauma and its powerful impact.

This handbook will explain how trauma is the source of the behavior that brings a girl to your attention; and why it is essential to incorporate, in policy and practice, a gender-responsive, trauma-informed approach throughout her continuum of care, if we are to successfully aid in her recovery, health and self-reliance.

It is our hope that this handbook will be a bridge that allows you to reach the girls in your program, so that with your help they might have a better future.

—Pam Patton
State and National Liaison and president for 20 years of the Oregon Coalition of Advocates for Equal Access for Girls

Why Should We Care About Trauma and Girls?

Introduction

Amy was 8 years old when her father was killed in an accident. The loss was devastating to her. Without her father, Amy's mother took a second job to keep them in their apartment, leaving little time for Amy. Then her mother met and married John. John was a divisive man who felt threatened by Amy's role in her mother's life. He was verbally abusive and when he drank too much he could become enraged, which frightened Amy. Sometimes while Amy's mother was at work, John would touch Amy sexually. Amy was afraid to tell anyone, and her grades and school participation began to falter. She became increasingly disconnected from her friends and teachers. It was difficult for Amy to concentrate. She felt alone and afraid, and unable to cope, and was drawn to the girls and boys around her who seemed to know her pain, or at least how to deaden it. Drugs were a way for her to be numb, and seemed the only escape from the fear and hopelessness that engulfed her…

Even though a girl who experiences trauma tries to cope and survive as best she can, trauma can redirect her onto an unhealthy and self-destructive path. And then there she is…in front of you. Lost. Distrustful. Scared. Reactive.

The encouraging news is that her life is more likely to be turned around if she comes in contact with a person or program that understands trauma and recognizes that trauma is the likely source of her behavior.

Her behavior brought her to your attention. Now the process begins, first with what trauma researchers refer to as universal precautions. This means all aspects of your program are grounded in the knowledge that a majority of system-involved girls have experienced traumatic events or are at risk of experiencing them.

A "trauma-informed" program or system:

- Integrates a trauma-informed approach
- Offers trauma-specific services
- Promotes healthy attachments
- Provides physical and emotional safety
- And supports trauma education and regulation skills

Achieving a trauma-informed program or system requires a cultural shift in your approach with girls; one that also includes an awareness of the impact a girl's trauma has on staff, who can experience vicarious trauma or secondary traumatic stress.

This handbook is for programs and people who work with girls, girls who have experienced trauma and its effects. Trauma is the driving force of the behaviors that put a girl on a path to your door. This handbook will explain why it is essential to integrate a trauma-informed, gender-responsive approach throughout a girl's continuum of care, in policy and practice, if we are to successfully aid in her healing and recovery.

Why is Trauma Important?

A majority of the girls in our programs have experienced interpersonal violence, sexual and physical abuse or domestic violence, or they have witnessed acts of violence, addiction, serious accidents, natural disaster, war, terrorism or political violence, personal peril and/or the loss of a loved one or caregiver.[1] Trauma is pervasive and it threads the fabric of their lives.

Girls who have experienced trauma often see themselves as fundamentally flawed and they can feel alone, without support, scrapping in the dark to survive in a dangerous world. Trauma profoundly shapes their lives and the paths they chose. After experiencing trauma, girls can see their options as limited and turn their reactions inward—causing increased problems in school, incidents of running away from home, suicide attempts, amplified mental health problems, anxiety and depression, escapist behavior through drugs or alcohol and/or engagement in other self-harming behaviors.

If only a girl's behavior and not her trauma is considered or addressed, you will see her previous non-productive behaviors repeat and continue.

While prevalent with boys, for girls trauma is endemic.[2]

Girls come to the attention of Juvenile Justice and the social services system differently than boys:

- A girl's first contact with Juvenile Justice or law enforcement is often for behavior that would not be considered criminal if committed by an adult.
- Girls frequently "visit" delinquency—through status offenses or misdemeanors, and therefore may only have a brief initial encounter.
- Girls rarely enter or end up in the Juvenile Justice system for violent or person-to-person crimes.
- If/when these girls go deeper into the system, it is often for violations of probation, not for more severe offenses[3]—unlike boys whose progression more often involves an escalation of offenses and reoffending.

When your program understands that it is the experience of trauma that most often brings a girl to your attention, you can then recognize needed changes in your intake, your approach with girls, your services, and the training necessary to succeed.

> *This awareness shift—understanding that a majority of girls involved in your system have experienced trauma, especially those encountering the Juvenile Justice or Child Welfare Systems—is the key to enhancing and empowering your program.*

Trauma impacts how girls view, approach and live their lives, and therefore how they will experience your program or system.

Your system's focus, during a girl's first contact, may traditionally be her specific conduct or situation—her offense in Juvenile Justice or her dependency in Child Welfare.

This initial contact may involve standardized forms and interview questions— your focus and strategy for a girl's intake being guided by the system's immediate mandates rather than the girl's holistic reality.

Asking trauma questions early in the girl's involvement with the Juvenile Justice or social services system can be challenging. First you must build a relationship with the girl, which requires taking time, being present, and creating a context of safety to restore power to her and build her self-worth. Then, once you've built a foundation of trust, trauma screening and assessment tools can be used to help guide your provided services and referrals.

To maximize your success, you don't need to change what you're doing, but how you're doing it. In the case of Juvenile Justice, this means an evolution in how we help girls be accountable and understand their world. So that in the process of coping with trauma girls do not reoffend—thereby keeping both the girl and the public safe.

The challenge posed to your program and all systems that serve girls is this: Make a cultural shift to using a trauma-informed and gender-responsive lens with girls at all levels and with all staff.

Doing so will offer you an essential advancement in practices and effectiveness: how you see a girl, how you relate to her, and how you will grow to understand her, her life and her behavior, so that she might heal, thrive on her own, and choose the healthy options before her.

The Impact of Trauma and Intersectionality on Girls

Girls differ from boys in their relationships, cultural roles, communication and learning styles, and in the prevalence of the types of trauma they experience.

Girls and boys are socialized differently, experience and respond to events differently, have different pathways to problem behaviors, and while facing similar challenges often face them differently.

Trauma can overwhelm the capacity for a girl to understand and integrate her experiences into her life. Trauma can create fear, powerlessness, dysfunction and helplessness, and it can lower a girl's feeling of self-worth.

Because of these differences, your strategies and approaches for girls need to be different. They need to be gender-responsive and they need to be trauma-informed.

Race/ethnicity, sexual orientation, gender identity and class also have a collective effect on how girls experience their social contexts, and in turn how they behave and relate to others and themselves. Intersectionality theory examines this interaction of different layers of identity and their effects on an individual's experiences.[4]

An awareness of intersectionality, and how it effects a girl's reality, is indispensable when shaping a girl's experience in the Juvenile Justice and Child Welfare system, and how the system responds to and affects girls' different identities.

Gender and race intersect to create categories of girls who are especially vulnerable to certain system policies and practices. Existing patterns of both sexism and racism collide in their effect on girls of color, increasing their chance of arrest and driving them deeper into the system. Girls of color may suffer a cumulative disadvantage based on historical traumas related to racism and poverty, layered with struggles stemming from recent traumatic experiences, family chaos, and environmental stress—common experiences for girls. It is therefore essential that intersectionality be understood and integrated when considering the impact of trauma on girls.[4]

Trauma-informed interventions support self-determination, and focus on empowerment, and helping girls to find and use their voice.

Trauma-informed programs for girls address the emotional and psychological aspects of trauma and ensure that girls reject the compulsion to believe that they are responsible for their abuse and victimization.[5]

When you understand trauma and its intersectional effect, your program can succeed for girls—by creating a safe, informed context for them, while restoring their power and value as individuals.

What is Meant by a *Program is Trauma-Informed?*

Definition: Trauma

A girl experiences trauma as a result to an event, series of events, or set of circumstances that is experienced by her as physically or emotionally harmful or life threatening. It can also be chronic or repeated circumstances or events. This result has lasting adverse effects on her functioning and mental, physical, social, emotional, and/or spiritual well-being. It can overwhelm her coping skills and cause a bio-chemical reaction and change her brain patterns.

Compared with adults, children exposed to trauma suffer increased negative and sustained effects — particularly when exposed to multiple types of traumatic events (poly-victimization), and even more so when on a repeated or chronic basis.

The term trauma has come to encompass a broad spectrum of experiences.

Types of Trauma

There are several types of trauma:

Acute Trauma—a single traumatic event that is limited in time such as an earthquake, car accident, dog bite, injury, sexual or physical assault, rape, witnessing abuse/violence, natural or human-made disasters, or the witness or experience of street violence.

Chronic Trauma—may refer to multiple and varied traumatic events such as a child who is exposed to domestic violence at home, emotional or psychological or sexual or physical abuse, neglect/abandonment, is disfigured in an accident and then bullied at school, or longstanding trauma such as experienced in a warzone or through historical or current oppression, structural violence (racism) or genocide.

Complex Trauma—describes both an exposure to multiple traumatic events, often of an invasive, interpersonal nature, and the wide-ranging, long-term impact of this exposure. These events are severe and pervasive, such as profound abuse or neglect. They usually begin early in life and can disrupt many aspects of development and the very formation of a self. It can include structural oppression or harm that is the result of our systems.

These above examples of traumatic events are not meant to be comprehensive. Trauma is very individual and is defined by the person who has the experience.

Definition: Trauma-Informed Approach and Trauma-Specific Services

A trauma-informed approach empowers your organizational culture and practices. More than what you do; it is how you do it.

A trauma-informed approach, like a gender-responsive approach is not an "add-on" to your program; it is a universal framework that requires specific changes to the practices, policies, and culture of your entire organization. It is providing all staff with the trauma and intersectionality awareness, knowledge and skills needed to successfully support girls.

Utilizing a *trauma-informed screening* at intake is a programmatic commitment that requires more than a checklist of forms and questions. It is assessing exactly what information you need to know about the girl and the availability of appropriate trauma-specific support and services to provide her. While performing an intake screening, you should ask yourself; will this information change the services you will provide? And more importantly, will it help the girl?

Your program needs to decide whether specific intake questions about the girl's trauma history will help her and improve your services; whether it is worth the risk of re-traumatizing the girl by asking questions at her intake about what kind of trauma she has experienced. And whether the information you will receive from the girl will be accurate or helpful.

Your understanding that most system-involved girls have experienced trauma may be enough to create an initial trust experience, without further detailed questioning, and thereby achieve a successful intake.

Your most important intake step is investing the time necessary, to allow a relationship of trust to develop with the girl.

> A trauma-informed intake includes your finesse, tone, and ability to explain why you're asking the questions you are. It is built upon your sensitivity to the girl's life experiences, and the intent behind the questions that you ask her. This means knowing that you are asking the right questions, and for the right reasons.

The foundation of all trauma-informed care services for girls is a commitment to trauma awareness and a knowledge of trauma recovery services.

This includes:

- Educating girls and staff
- Your hiring and supervision practices
- Policies and procedures at intake and throughout your system
- And most importantly a system-wide understanding of the impact past trauma experiences have on girls

Trauma-specific services and assessments are clinical interventions that are designed to address trauma related symptoms. They are done by professional staff members, and begin with a systemic knowledge of the impact that trauma has on girls' lives and behavior.

To provide effective *trauma-specific services* for girls, your system must use treatment methods that will remediate symptoms associated with traumatic stress, promote healing and recovery, build protection and resilience, and address functional deficits.

Therapeutic services and all contract services need to be provided by staff who have been educated about girls (gender) and trauma, and trained to incorporate a trauma-informed approach in their work.

> **Substance Abuse and Mental Health Services Administration (SAMHSA) defines a trauma-informed framework using the "Four R's":**
> 1. **R**ealize the impact of trauma on girls and staff
> 2. **R**ecognize the signs of trauma
> 3. **R**espond to the girl and staff trauma
> 4. **R**esist re-traumatizing

Principles of a Trauma-Informed Approach— a "Trauma Lens"

A trauma-informed approach is a knowledge and culture shift that requires staff to use a "trauma lens" and a "gender lens" while working with girls.

Through a *gender lens*, staff are aware of and acknowledge female physical, emotional, psychological development and girls' social contexts and environments in all that they do.

While there is overlap among the adverse social contexts or environments that coexist in boys and girls, research suggests that due to girls' unique development and socialization they can be more vulnerable to certain negative outcomes from their social contexts and environments. For many girls, adversity in their home, communities, and in the way they experience society is traumatizing.[6]

Staff also need to assume that a significant majority of the girls in their program have experienced some form of trauma, and be sensitive to that fact as to how the program is structured and presented.

A trauma lens acknowledges trauma occurred but does not allow it to "define" the girl.

A trauma-informed approach needs to:

Take the trauma into account, as a fundamental impact on the girl.

Avoid triggering trauma reactions, and/or re-traumatizing the girl.

Adjust the behavior of staff, to support the girl's coping capacity.

Allow survivors to manage their trauma symptoms successfully;
so that they can access, retain and benefit from the services.[7]

A trauma-informed approach is strength-based and understands the impact of trauma on girls' lives and sets up physical and psychological safety for them while providing opportunities to rebuild personal power and control over their lives and future.

Using a gender and trauma lens while providing a trauma-informed approach enhances the probability of a successful outcome for girls.

Through this approach staff:

Create a safe context (physically and emotionally safe; with transparency, predictability, and clear and consistent boundaries with staff)

Restore personal power (give girls choices, empowerment, internal strength, skills building, and modeling)

And value the individual girl (through respect, authenticity, collaboration, compassion, mutuality, and relationship)[8]

Some girls appear to have greater resiliency or post trauma growth following exposure to a traumatic event while others may experience a wide range of possible clinical trauma disorders.

A traumatized girl coming to the attention of Juvenile Justice or Child Welfare staff may display one or more of the following:

- Aggression • Anger • Anxiety • Conduct Disorder • Depression
- Distrust • Hyper-Arousal • Impaired Information Processing
- Impulse Control Problems • Oppositional-Defiant Behavior
- Problems With Personal Boundaries • Sleep Problems
- Somatic Complaints • Substance Use • Suicide Ideation and/or Attempts

> The National Center for Mental Health and Juvenile Justice suggests using a trauma-informed screening, assessment and then treatment of girls coming to the attention of the Juvenile Justice system, through the establishment of a continuum of services and collaboration across youth service providers, including behavioral health, education, and child protection.

There are four generally accepted principles in the trauma-informed care (approach) field:[9]

1. **Trauma Awareness:** Those who are trauma-informed will understand the prevalence and impact of trauma among their service recipients and within the workforce. Policy and practice reflect this awareness and may be supported with activities such as screening and assessments.

2. **Safety:** Policy and practice reflect a commitment to provide physical and emotional safety for service recipients and staff.

3. **Choice and Empowerment:** To facilitate healing and avoid re-traumatization, choice and empowerment are part of trauma informed service delivery, for both service recipients and staff.

4. **Strengths Based:** With a focus on strength and resilience, service recipients and staff build skills that will help them move in a positive direction.

In essence, a program that is trauma-informed acknowledges and sees the widespread impact of trauma, and understands potential paths to help a girl lead a healthy, productive life, and avoids re-traumatization; it recognizes the signs and symptoms of trauma in girls and responds with a fully integrated trauma-informed approach in all services/policies and practices.

SAMHSA has identified seven principles of trauma-informed services and systems:

1. Safety
2. Trustworthiness
3. Empowerment, Voice and Choice
4. Collaboration and Mutuality
5. Peer Support
6. Cultural, Historical, and Gender issues
7. Family Engagement, Empowerment and Collaboration

For girls' programs to reach their stated mission, they must first understand the factors that impact and affect the lives of the girls in their programs, the most common and serious underlying factor of which is exposure to trauma.

The National Council of Juvenile and Family Court Judges identifies 10 things important to know for trauma-informed services:

1. A traumatic experience is an event that threatens someone's life, safety or well-being.
2. Child traumatic stress can lead to Post Traumatic Stress Disorder (PTSD).
3. Trauma impacts a child's development and health throughout his or her life.
4. Complex trauma is associated with risk of delinquency.
5. Traumatic exposure, delinquency and school failure are related.
6. Trauma assessments can reduce misdiagnosis, promote outcomes and maximize resources.
7. There are mental health treatments that are effective in helping youth who are experiencing child traumatic stress.
8. There is a compelling need for effective family involvement.
9. Youth are resilient.
10. **Next steps:** *The Juvenile Justice system needs to be trauma-informed at all levels.*

Trauma Exposure

Profile Data

Justice-involved youth experience trauma at rates that are eight times higher than community samples.[10]

There are important gender differences related to the prevalence of trauma, its impact, and the treatment needs of girls and boys, which require gender-specific approaches.

- Over 70% of girls experience trauma in general and more frequently report sexual and physical abuse compared to boys.[11]

- Generally, there is a national trend of declining arrest rates for youth. However, from 1996-2011 girls arrest rates declined less than did boys arrest rates (42 percent versus 57 percent). From 2003-2012, arrests of boys for simple assault declined by 32 percent, while arrests of girls for the same offense declined by only 19 percent. For property crimes, arrests of boys declined 39 percent, but only 29 percent for girls. *The forces that are driving arrest rates down for boys are not affecting girls in an equitable way.*

- 85% of all urban youth and 61% of rural youth have experienced community violence. For girls, community violence is linked to sexual harassment and consequent feelings of sexual vulnerability in their communities. Many girls live in "coercive sexual environments"— communities where harassment, domestic violence, and sexual exploitation are a part of everyday life and are even normalized. In poor, distressed communities, both girls and boys are subject to violence related to gangs and drug trafficking; *but girls additionally suffer traumatic effects from sexual harassment and violence, and live in constant fear.*

- Girls who are exposed to community violence—as both victims and witnesses—have higher rates than boys of PTSD (post-traumatic stress disorder), depression, anxiety, and substance use, often co-occurring with one another.

While justice-involved girls and boys both have high rates of trauma in general, more girls meet the criteria for Post-Traumatic Stress Disorder (PTSD) than boys.[12]

Girls are also more likely to have strong psychological responses to experiencing or witnessing trauma, where boys are more likely to be affected by experiencing trauma vs. witnessing it.[13]

Adverse Childhood Experiences (ACE) Study

The Adverse Childhood Experiences (ACE) Study, originally funded by the Center for Disease Control—Kaiser Permanente, showed how childhood trauma is linked to mental, behavioral and physical outcomes. For instance, it impacts the adult onset of chronic disease, mental illness, violence and being a victim of violence. It measured 10 types of childhood adversity, those that occurred before the age of 18. They are physical, verbal and sexual abuse; physical and emotional neglect; a family member with mental illness, or who has been incarcerated, or is abusing alcohol or other drugs; witnessing a mother being abused; losing a parent to divorce or separation.

Of the 17,337 mostly white, college-educated people with jobs and private health care who participated in the study, 64 percent had an ACE score of one or more; 12 percent had an ACE score of four or more (i.e., four out of the 10 different types of adversity).

The researchers found that the higher a person's ACE score, the greater the risk of chronic disease, mental illness and anti-social/criminal behavior. For example, compared with someone who has an ACE score of zero, a person with an ACE score of four or more is twice as likely to smoke, 12 times more likely to attempt suicide, seven times more likely to become an alcoholic, 10 times more likely to have injected street drugs, and twice as likely to have heart disease. People with a score of six or higher have shorter lifespans—20 years shorter. The cumulative effect is profound. The study revealed a hidden epidemic: *Adverse Childhood Experiences (ACE's) contribute to most of our major chronic health, mental health, economic health and social health issues.*

The ACE Study is one part of a new understanding that's sometimes called "the unified science" of human development. The five parts of this ACEs science include the epidemiology of childhood adversity (ACE Study), how *toxic stress from childhood trauma can damage the structure and function of a child's developing brain* (neurobiology of toxic stress), how *toxic stress embeds in a person's biology to emerge decades later as disease* (biomedical consequences of toxic stress), how the effects of *toxic stress can be passed from parent to child and generation to generation* (epigenetics), and how resilience research is showing how the brain is plastic and the body wants to heal.

Conversely, research has emerged on resilience that has shown exercise, nutrition, being in a safe relationship, (for a child) being in a relationship with a trusted adult, living in a safe place, and mindfulness all contribute to a healthy brain and body. Resilience research also covers organization, system and community resilience—such as how *trauma-informed, resilience-building schools and programs help students with high ACE scores increase their grades, test scores, graduation rates, sense of well-being, and hope for the future.*

Girls in your programs have most likely experienced trauma multiple times. It was not a single event.

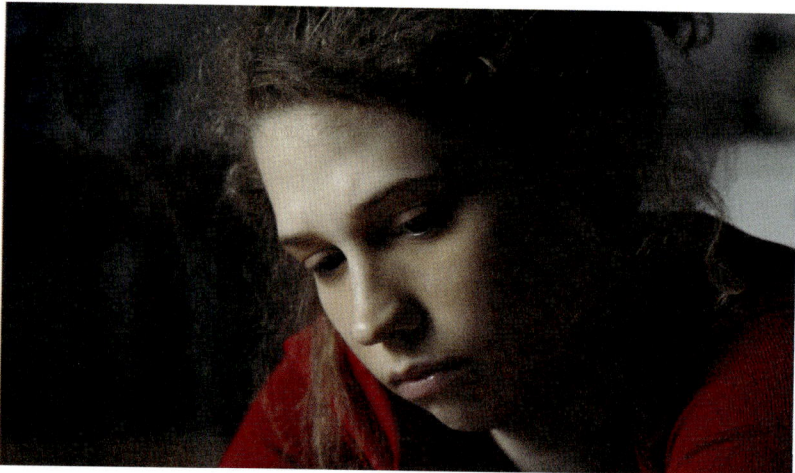

The National Crittenton Foundation's (TNCF) 2014-15 Administration of the ACE survey, demographic questions, and well-being questions was implemented at 18 of the Crittenton family of agencies and found that:

- TNCF female and male survey respondents have significantly higher ACE scores than respondents in both the original Kaiser Permanente-CDC ACE study and the Philadelphia Urban ACE study.

- TNCF female respondents have higher ACE scores than TNCF male respondents particularly in the ACE score range of eight to 10.

- TNCF females have higher prevalence of individual ACEs than males, and females have a higher prevalence of individual ACEs across all ACE categories. However, the largest differences are for sexual abuse (32% difference), emotional neglect (21% difference), and provider care mental illness (16%).

- Females with ACE scores of four or more who are in the foster care system experience more placement instability. The number of placements nearly doubled when comparing those who scored four–seven, to those who scored eight–10.

- A significant percentage of girls and young women receiving residential treatment services have high ACE scores. Not surprisingly, 65% of TNCF females in residential treatment have ACE scores of four or more, including 27% with scores of eight or more. These scores suggest trauma histories that make residential treatment an essential component of their treatment plan.

- Females with at least one child, or parents who had their first pregnancy as teens, have high ACE scores.

- Children of respondents have significant ACE histories before age 10.

Additionally, a recent study of Adverse Childhood Experiences among 64,300 youth involved in the Florida Juvenile Justice system indicates that the experiences of boys and girls varies in terms of exposure to traumatic events. The researchers compared the prevalence of the ACE indicators by gender and found that females reported a higher prevalence rate on every indicator, with the most striking distinction being sexual abuse, which was reported 4.4 times more frequently by females than males.

The Impact of Trauma on the Brain

When a person experiences trauma, the survival reactions of fight, flight or freeze take over. The "amygdala" (the part of the brain that detects fear and prepares for emergency events) becomes over-developed.

The frontal lobe, which controls planning for the future, judgment, decision-making skills, attention span, and inhibition is under-developed and therefore is harder to bring on-line when the amygdala is working so hard. But, healing/recovery and "re-wiring" is possible.

Every girl reacts to trauma in her own way. However, some typical reactions include:

- Emotional Reactions (hyper-vigilance, overly emotional)
- Psychological and Cognitive Reactions (difficulty concentrating, slowed thinking, difficulty with decisions, blame)
- Behavioral or Physical (sleep disturbance, substance abuse, frequently ill—especially GI tract problems, pain)
- Beliefs and Values (difficulty trusting anyone, lowered self-worth and of others, difficulty in relationships)

Now, using what you've learned at this point in the handbook, look at these common situations using a gender-lens and trauma-lens. Do they seem any different to you?

- A girl doesn't tell you the truth.
- A girl makes an appointment but doesn't show up or if she does, she doesn't seem engaged.
- A girl seems inattentive or spacey. She has difficulty remembering whether or not she has done something.
- A girl complains that the program is unfair, that she is being targeted unfairly.
- A girl is combative with authority figures.
- A girl changes her mind about what she wants or can't make up her mind.

Being aware of how these behaviors may be connected to traumatic experiences is a first step toward developing a systemic trauma-informed approach for girls that works.

Trauma and Risk Behavior

Research consistently demonstrates a strong relationship between trauma and problem behaviors, especially among girls.[14]

For the girls in your programs, the impact of trauma may reveal itself as:[15]

- Lack of basic trust, fearfulness and low self-esteem
- Loss of emotional management and inability to integrate experiences
- Interpersonal communication breakdowns and relational conflicts
- Isolation, not working together with others, indifference and detachment
- Repeating familiar patterns even if they don't work or are destructive
- Loss of creative problem-solving ability and loss of interest in participating
- Choosing silence instead of dissent and learned helplessness
- Hostile, reactive, defensive and avoidant attitudes or responses

Re-Traumatization

Common practices in the Juvenile Justice system and in some girls' programs can re-traumatize girls who have experienced trauma.

Many triggers revolve around relationships and physical contact.

For example, these actions could be triggers. Try to avoid or be sensitive to:

- Loud voices, yelling, brusque orders
- Unsafe environments
- Walking up behind a girl, surprises
- Any touching
- Demeaning names
- Sexual jokes or casual comments about a girl's body, and/or her situation
- Discussing trauma or mental health incidents in open court
- Posturing, power struggles
- Disrobing
- Physical exams
- Strip searches
- Body cavity searches
- Take downs, being strapped to bed, restrained
- Shower observations by staff

Preparing Your Program to be Trauma-Informed

Assessing Trauma-Informed Standards with the G-SAT

One way to determine if your program is both gender-responsive to girls and trauma-informed is to compare it to best practices.

The Oregon Coalition of Advocates for Equal Access for Girls developed guidelines for girls' programs to help them be more gender-responsive. The *Gender-Responsive Standards and Assessment Tool* ("G-SAT") was designed to improve the quality and nature of services provided to girls, thereby increasing girl's chances for success and self-sufficiency. The G-SAT was refined, piloted with staff and girls, and developed into 59 best practices standards for residential programs for girls (2011), 45 best practices standards for therapeutic/treatment foster care (2013), and 56 best practices standards for community programs (2016). Each G-SAT has two tools: one for staff/foster parents and one for the girls to complete.

The G-SAT includes approximately 11 standards that specifically address trauma. All the standards reinforce one another through clear and consistent systemic gender-responsive programming for girls and young women. The standards are not intended to be all-inclusive, but rather serve as a catalyst encouraging professionals to look critically at how services are provided to girls. All the standards are interconnected and build on each other to create an environment that can enhance and maximize program effectiveness for girls.

Agency/Program/Staff Readiness: Training and Culture

To ensure your agency's readiness to incorporate a gender-responsive/trauma-informed approach for girls, it is important to look at two things: staff training and program culture.

1. A Well-trained Staff

- A program that has integrated a trauma-informed approach trains new staff by well-trained staff's example. Be clear who you want your program staff to be. For example, staff need to be secure, healthy adults with good emotional management skills; have the ability to teach and be role models and be empathetic yet have good boundaries; are patient and understanding yet structured enough for security and safety; have the ability to endure intense, emotional situations on a daily basis. You want staff that do not abuse power. Additionally, staff need to learn the skills necessary for working with traumatized youth/girls (i.e., de-escalation, safety planning). A beginning place might be the SAMHSA training, *Think Trauma: A Training for Staff in Juvenile Justice Residential Settings,* a PowerPoint®-based training curriculum including four modules that can be implemented back-to-back in a single day training or in four consecutive training sessions over the course of several weeks or months. More information at equalaccessforgirls.org/think-trauma. New staff should receive training immediately on your trauma-informed approach. Ongoing (booster) trainings should occur regularly.

- Establish a staff vicarious/secondary trauma training using mental health professionals. There are training materials available through SAMHSA and other resources listed at the end of this handbook. Let staff know there are resources and support staff to help them cope with the trauma they have experienced in their own lives or from working with girls who have experienced trauma.

2. A Trauma-Informed, Supportive Program Culture

- Your agency or program culture is an expression of your values. It can be seen in the way staff and girls behave, the "energy" in the room, the relationships, and atmosphere. It can be tangible and intangible things, informal and formal policies and practices. Culture influences all activities and services. It penetrates throughout groups of administrators, supervisors, direct services staff, support staff and the girls themselves.

- Culture impacts the effectiveness of program services and therefore needs to be examined—where is the resistance and where is the support—when preparing for your program to be trauma-informed. The program culture needs to be open to learning and change.

Trauma-informed services can change a program's culture to one that is more responsive and much more effective. It is a better way to do the work because it gets to the core of girls' issues—that brought them to the program. The core trauma issues can be visited, unpacked, and redirected.

A trauma-informed culture doesn't ignore trauma. It helps take away its power. For the culture to change, all staff, from the top down and bottom up, need to buy into providing a trauma-informed approach and trauma-informed services—thus maximizing the chances for a girl to reach her full potential.

Trauma-informed Screening and Assessment Tools for Girls

Selecting a Tool

The following screening and assessment tools are for consideration and should not be viewed as a recommendation. Since each program for girls is unique, staff will need to determine what best meets the needs of the girls they are serving, what the goal is for the screening and when to decide if a girl needs an assessment by a mental health professional.

Information on tools can be found *below*.

Most assessment tools used by programs at intake are designed for all youth (not specifically girls). Additionally, attention to past trauma varies among tools. To be more comprehensive and responsive to girls' trauma and needs, some programs use a combination of tools. For instance, a program might administer an intake tool and use it in conjunction with the 10 questions on the Adverse Childhood Experiences (ACE) questionnaire—such as what was discussed earlier with the Crittenton Foundation study. Some programs will decide not to use either at intake.

The developers of the MAYSI-2 tool at the University of Massachusetts, the most widely used screening tool in Juvenile Justice in the US, includes a traumatic experiences scale but is not specifically a "trauma screen." Jonathan C. Clayfield, MA, LMHC, Project Director, Law & Psychiatry Program—Research in Juvenile Justice, Psychiatry Department, University of Massachusetts Medical School stated that *"they haven't come across any trauma screening tools that are specifically for screening justice-involved girls."*

(At the bottom of page 34 is a link to an article by Dr. Wevodau comparing 11 validated trauma screening tools for youth.)

The following action steps are recommended for programs to determine how to proceed with using an effective *gender-responsive trauma-informed intake screening/ assessment tool*:

Step 1: Establish the Purpose of the Tool

An important first step is to establish a tool selection *criterion*. That is, identify the goal and specific purpose for the tool, what you specifically wish to address (what is the current gap/problem) and what you want to measure (e.g., PTSD, exposure to trauma, symptoms of past trauma, mental health issues, physical issues related to trauma).

When considering various strategies for identifying girls exposed to trauma or who may be experiencing a trauma-related disorder, it is important to understand the *purpose* for asking the question before you can determine which strategy is *best*. There are several trauma screening tools for youth but they each identify different types of trauma and the impact of trauma.

For additional information on how to select a trauma screening tool and important aspects to consider, the articles below offer a good starting place as you formulate your context and purpose for your tool selection.

Identifying Dual Status Youth with Trauma-Related Problems:
equalaccessforgirls.org/identifying-youth-trauma

Trauma in Dual Status Youth: Putting Things In Perspective:
equalaccessforgirls.org/youth-trauma-perspective

Additionally, the National Child Traumatic Stress Network (nctsnet.org) offers resources on Screening and Assessment in the Juvenile Justice System, including a webinar entitled: "*The Need for Trauma-Informed Screening and Assessment in Juvenile Justice Settings: Strengths and Limitations of Commonly Used Instruments*" (2012) by Carly Drekhising, UCLA and Patricia Kerig, Ph.D. University of Utah.

Step 2: Determine if you want a Screening Tool or an Assessment Tool

Some programs for girls may wish to use a universal approach and identify the presence or absence of trauma-related problems for every girl with whom you come in contact. If so, *trauma screening tools* can serve that purpose. They take a relatively short amount of time to administer; therefore, it is feasible for them to be given to every girl entering a program.

However, trauma screening tools do not provide definitive diagnoses. Instead, they serve a triage function to determine the need for more detailed information and services. Again, the information's accuracy will depend on where the girl is at and how skilled the interviewer is in creating a safe relationship-based environment.

In contrast to screening tools, *trauma assessment tools* are designed to facilitate staff in gaining a more definitive, comprehensive, and individualized picture of a girl, which will be useful in developing an intervention plan. That is, these tools often offer a clearer picture of the specific nature of a girl's individual needs. Juvenile Justice services using these tools must have qualified mental health professionals on staff to administer and interpret them.

Step 3: Compare the Pros and Cons of Existing Tools

In the article *Review of Trauma Screening Tools for Children and Adolescents* (January 2016) by Amy Wevodau, Ph.D., Law and Psychiatry Program, University of Massachusetts Medical School (see link below for full article), Dr. Wevodau compares the top 11 trauma screening instruments for youth and discusses the pros and cons of each tool, cost, time to administer and score, who should administer the tool, demographics, reading level, what they can and can't measure, target groups, validity and reliability, etc.

equalaccessforgirls.org/review-of-trauma-screenings

Examples of the 11 Trauma Screening and Assessment Tools for Youth

Dr. Amy Wevodau identified 11 currently available screening tools that provide information about trauma in children and adolescents. *A majority of tools are not gender-specific, however, or validated on girls.*

The 11 tools fall into three categories:

A. *Exposure*—whether a youth has been exposed to traumatic events

B. *PTSD*—whether that exposure has led to a specific trauma-relevant disorder, Posttraumatic Stress Disorder (PTSD)

C. *Trauma-related Symptoms*—whether the youth might have any of a variety of psychological symptoms often related to previous traumatic experiences

The following is a list of the 11 trauma tools that fall into these three categories. The tools themselves may be found through the link above (or an on-line search).

A. *Tools that Measure Exposure to Trauma:* Tools that screen for degree and/or type of exposure to events that have the potential to be traumatizing.

   1. Juvenile Victimization Questionnaire (JVQ)
   2. Survey of Children's Exposure to Community Violence (SCECV)
   3. Traumatic Events Screening Inventory (TESI)

According to the DSM-5, a traumatic event involves exposure to, witnessing of, or learning of actual or threatened death, serious injury or physical violence toward one's self or a loved one. These tools can be useful if a program's goal includes identifying youth who are at risk of having a trauma-related disorder or developing one in the future.

Some of the tools in this category also offer information about specific features of exposure, frequency and whether there has been exposure to multiple types of traumatic event exposures (i.e., poly-victimization). However, one must be clear about their limits. They will not indicate whether youth have developed trauma-related symptoms or a trauma-related disorder. They are of value in raising a flag for further assessment, but do not offer a basis for deciding on application of a trauma-based intervention.

In addition, the Massachusetts Youth Screening Instrument-Version 2 (MAYSI-2), a brief mental health screening tool for adolescents, contains a scale for *Traumatic Experiences* among its seven scales. Many agencies also use the Adverse Childhood Experiences (ACE) tool, which is described earlier in this handbook and can be added to gain a better understanding of the youth's history and exposure to potentially harmful experiences in childhood.

B. **Tools that Measure PTSD Symptoms:** Tools that screen for symptoms of Post-Traumatic Stress Disorder.

4. Child PTSD Symptom Scale (CPSS)
5. Los Angeles Symptoms Checklist (LASC)
6. Structured Trauma-Related Experiences and Symptoms Screener (STRESS)
7. University of California at Los Angeles Posttraumatic Stress Disorder Reaction Index (UCLA PTSD-RI)

These tools typically present youth with a list of symptoms consistent with DSM-5 criteria for Post-Traumatic Stress Disorder and ask youth to indicate which symptoms they have experienced during a given time period. Scoring rules built into the tool or identified by prior research with the tool then allow one to identify the likelihood that the youth will be found to have PTSD if given a more thorough assessment.

These tools are useful for deciding which youth should be referred for actual diagnostic assessment specifically for PTSD, in contrast to youth who have been exposed but are less likely to have developed PTSD as a consequence. Even when the youth does not reach the criterion for "likely" PTSD, examining PTSD-like symptoms that the youth displays can be helpful in considering referral for a diagnostic assessment and thinking about a youth's treatment needs.

C. **Tools that Measure Trauma-Related Symptoms:** Tools that screen for a range of symptoms often associated with trauma, but not specifically for the cluster of symptoms associated with Post-Traumatic Stress Disorder as a psychiatric diagnostic construct.

8. Adolescent Dissociative Experiences Scale (A-DES)
9. Child and Adolescent Psychiatric Assessment (CAPA)
10. Child Report of Post-Traumatic Symptoms (CROPS) and Parent Report of Post-Traumatic Symptoms (PROPS)
11. Trauma Symptom Checklist for Children (TSCC)

These tools screen for the presence of mental health symptoms that may be caused by or related to trauma, but which are not captured by measures focused solely on PTSD. These may include, for example, depression, problems with anger, and difficulties in relationships. Therefore, tools in this category may be useful to services interested in understanding the potential range of mental health problems faced by youth who have experienced trauma.

Given their diverse focus, the structure of these tools can vary greatly. However, one of their primary benefits lies in their ability to screen for complex trauma reactions such as difficulties across multiple areas (e.g., significant problems regulating emotions, disrupted attachments). Youth may also present with an altered sense of self and future, physical distress and an overdeveloped avoidance response that might lead to dissociation, substance abuse, or self-injurious behavior. Therefore, tools that screen for a range of symptoms (not just those associated with PTSD), may provide a more complete picture of the difficulties experienced by some traumatized youth.

NOTE: There are a number of health-related tools that include some mention of trauma and abuse, yet are not included in the 11 tools mentioned above.

For example:

- The *Girls' Health Screen* by Leslie Acoca, Girls Health and Justice Institute, has a validated instrument in English and Spanish for girls ages 11-17. It focuses on health and mental health (abuse/trauma is referenced in that section).

- The National Center for Crime and Delinquency (NCCD) has JAIS, gender-specific assessment system that is to design and assess risk, strength, needs, and intervention strategies for girls.

- The April 2010 Girls' Study Group Report from NCJRS/OJJDP has an article *Suitability of Assessment Instruments for Delinquent Girls* by Susan Brumbaugh, Jennifer Hardison Walters and Laura Winterfield. They found 53 youth mental health assessment instruments that were "favorable to gender-based performance."

Resources

National Child Traumatic Stress Network
www.nctsn.org

SAMHSA National Center for Trauma Informed Care
www.samhsa.gov/nctic/

The National Crittenton Foundation's *Beyond ACE Issue Brief*
http://nationalcrittenton.org/wp-content/uploads/2016/09/ACE_REPORT_
finalsm.pdf

Trauma-Informed Oregon
"Standards of Practice for Trauma-Informed Care"
http://traumainformedoregon.org/standards-practice-trauma-informed-care/

Center for Gender and Justice
Opportunities for Implementing Trauma-Informed Practices for Girls' Facilities.
Checklist adapted by Candice Norcott, from Stephanie Covington and
Barbara Bloom's adaption of "National Resource Center on Justice-Involved
Women. 2014. *Using trauma-informed practices to enhance safety and security
in women's correctional facilities: Research Brief.* Silver Spring, MD: Author."

equalaccessforgirls.org/trauma-informed-practices-for-facilities

Endnotes

1   Baglivio, Michael T., et al., US Dept. of Justice, Office of Justice Programs, Office of Juvenile Justice & Delinquency Prevention, *The Prevelence of Adverse Childhood Experiences (ACE) in the Lives of Juvenile Offenders* (Spring 2014)

2   Baglivio, Michael T., et al., US Dept. of Justice, Office of Justice Programs, Office of Juvenile Justice & Delinquency Prevention, *The Prevelence of Adverse Childhood Experiences (ACE) in the Lives of Juvenile Offenders* (Spring 2014)

3   Sherman, Francine, & Annie Balck, *Gender Injustice, System Level Juvenile Justice Reforms for Girls*, (2015) (pg. 11)

4   Sherman, Francine, & Annie Balck, *Gender Injustice, System Level Juvenile Justice Reforms for Girls*, (2015) (pg. 22)

5   Briere J. & Scott C. (2006). *Principles of trauma therapy: A guide to symptoms, evaluations, and treatment.* Thousand Oaks, CA: Sage Publications

6   Sherman, Francine, & Annie Balck, *Gender Injustice, System Level Juvenile Justice Reforms for Girls*, (2015) (pg. 20)

7   Covington S. & Bloom, B. (2003), *Gendered Justice: Women in the criminal justice system.* In B. Bloom, ed, *Gendered Justice: Addressing Female Offenders*, NC: Carolina Academic Press. Harris, M. and Fallot, R.D. (Eds.), (2001)

8   Sherman, Francine, & Annie Balck, *Gender Injustice, System Level Juvenile Justice Reforms for Girls*, (2015)

9   Hopper, E.K., Bassuk, E.L., Olivet, J. (2010) Shelter from the Storm: Trauma-Informed Care in Homelessness Services Settings.

10 Wolpaw, J.W., & Ford, J.D. (2004). *Assessing exposure to psychological trauma stress in the Juvenile Justice population.* National Child Traumatic Stress Network, www.NCTSNet.org

11 Brosky and Lally, 2004. Cauffman et al.,1998; Mueser and Taub, 2008; NCCD Center for Girls and Young Women, *Understanding Trauma through a Gender Lens*; http://www.nccdglobal.org/sites/default/files/publication_pdf/understanding-trauma.pdf

12 Abram, K.M., et al, (2004), *Posttraumatic stress disorder and trauma in youth in juvenile detention.* Archives of General Psychiatry, 61, 403-401.

13 Foster, J.D., Kuperminc, G.P., Price A.W., (2004). *Gender differences in posttraumatic stress and related symptoms among inner-city minority youth exposed to community violence.* Journal of Youth and Adolescence, 33,59-69.

14 Chesney-Lind 1989. *Girls' Crime and Woman's Place: Toward a Feminist Model of Female Delinquency.* Crime and Delinquency 35, 5-29. Simkins, S, & Katz, S. (2002). *Criminalizing abused girls.* Violence Against Women, 8, 1919-1927.

15 Diane Yatchmenoff, Ph.D., Regional Research Institute, Portland State University (Oregon). (2015). http://traumainformedoregon.org/standards-practice-trauma-informed-care. *Trauma Informed Care- An Introduction* (PPT). Presentation at the 2015 Oregon Forensic Conference.

Made in the USA
Lexington, KY
12 May 2018